WALKING
WITH A
LIMP

WALKING
WITH A
LIMP

By Brad Bell

To request additional information, book speaking engagements or
request bulk purchase pricing, go to anatomyofadisciple.com.

ISBN# 978-0-9913061-0-7

Printed in the United States of America

To the broken,

who, like Jacob, walk with a limp to this day

ACKNOWLEDGMENTS

I would like to thank Dr. Rick Taylor, a friend and mentor, whose gentleness and knowledge of the scriptures have shaped my life beyond measure. For more than 20 years, Rick has wrestled with the issue of spiritual formation. His expertise, combined with the passion of a superbly talented staff team, created The Anatomy of a Disciple. Together, this team has forever changed my view of discipleship and spiritual formation. For a deeper understanding of The Anatomy of a Disciple, you can pick up Rick's book, "The Anatomy of a Disciple: So Many Believers. So Few Disciples."

I am grateful for the input and initiative of the pastoral staff at The Well Community Church. To Shea Sumlin, Jerrod Rumley, Dave Obwald, Chris Schultz, Andrew Feil, Scott Carolan, Greg Zuffelato and P.J. Lewis: you have exemplified the value of team and affirmed that we are truly better together than any of us would be alone. These men have field-tested the concepts with individuals and groups, and affirmed the credibility of The Anatomy of a Disciple, one changed life at a time.

Special thanks to Karen Price, my editor, for helping me find my voice. She pushed for provocative and unguarded content as my bride and I sat with her week after week over coffee; I will never look at my back porch the same. Together, we dug, argued and created a book true to my heart, and I'm convinced it is better because of her dogged persistence.

I can never adequately thank my bride, Jen, my best friend, faithful companion and ministry partner for years. Her patience created space for me to sneak away and write. She cheered me on when words came easy and provided much needed encouragement when the cursor blinked in mocking repetition when no words could be found. "Many women have done excellently, but you surpass them all" (Proverbs 31:29).

TABLE OF CONTENTS

FOREWORD

by Trent Dilfer

An MVP at Fresno State, sixth overall pick in the 1994 National Football League Draft by the Tampa Bay Buccaneers, 1997 Pro Bowl selection, and having earned a Super Bowl ring in Super Bowl XXXV with the Baltimore Ravens, former football quarterback Trent Dilfer is currently an NFL analyst for ESPN.

At training camp in college, I immediately gravitated toward Brad. He was the only guy out there that looked like me. And we were wired the same way. We both came from incredible dysfunction, carried huge chips on our shoulders, and went after anything with blonde hair and long legs. So deeply insecure, and full of youthful bravado to compensate, we played hard and partied hard. It was a beautifully dysfunctional relationship as we competed to see who could be the bigger mess. We were destructive, obsessive compulsive, and always looking for the next fix. In between football, we would work out like freaks, pick up hobbies, and we both dated my wife, Cass, the best-looking girl in school. We went full tilt in everything we did, and he was as crazy as I was.

So when I finally decided to get serious about living my faith, I knew we had to get him.

• • •

I went off to Tampa, scared to death, while Brad went to Dallas for seminary. I felt like I was living this dream in the world's eye, but never felt like I was doing the Lord's work. I didn't know how to weave my spiritual gifts into football. So I lived vicariously through Brad. I supported him. He was doing great stuff; he was doing what I thought I should have been doing.

He has sat with me in walnut fields talking life over a six-pack of Corona. He has taught my girls and I how to two-step before the daddy-daughter dance. He drove my wife and I to Stanford Hospital, following an ambulance carrying my 5-year-old son. He helped set up "Camp Trev," and never left for 40 days. And he stood by my side at Trevin's memorial.

Brad was a difference maker in my life, and I knew the Lord could really use him in others. I knew it then on the football field at Fresno State, and I know it today.

"Walking With A Limp" is going to change the way you pursue Christ and the way you live day to day. Brad is purposely transparent, using language that will reach you right where you're at. Page after page, he pushes for self-awareness in such a way that doesn't accuse you or make you feel like a loser.

He talks about the Core of your spiritual life, the engine that drives everything else. I call the Core: the lonely work. It's the planks for 30 minutes, Pilates or stretching. And no one wants to do the lonely work. They do curls for the girls. So much time is spent on the pretty parts. So much time is spent on what the world thinks of the outer layer. How tall, how big, how high, how fast they are. It's all surface. It's all about the touchdown catch, and no one talks about the block that got the first down that made the touchdown possible.

When the Lord finally broke me in the summer of 92, I wanted to quit living this half-in-half-out life. As I look back at my spiritual life over the last 21 years, I'm frustrated that I'm not stronger. Why am I not where I should be? I've learned choices are a direct result of the lonely work. So maybe, my lonely work hasn't been quite as lonely.

At the edge of uncomfortable is where you find greatness. That is where you are the most vulnerable. If you're willing to go there, and this book will help you get there, you will find greatness in your walk with God.

CHAPTER 1

JUST ANOTHER SUNDAY

I WAS SLEEPING WITH my girlfriend and going to church. I was living with my girlfriend and memorizing scripture. I was getting drunk at frat parties and doing steroids and all the while participating in accountability groups.

Jesus said, "He who is forgiven much, loves much."[1] I guess you could say I love much. I was a defensive lineman at Fresno State, graduating with a degree in Community Health Education, which for the record has been relatively worthless in my role as a pastor. I came to faith in Christ in college and spent a year and a half going through a 12-week Bible study called Operation

---

1 Personal translation of Luke 7:47

3

Timothy and sinned again and again. I would cry myself to sleep. I thought after I became a Christian my struggles would diminish. Didn't you?

You're supposed to pray and discover all this spiritual stuff, but you pray and it's summed up in 30 seconds of random thoughts and distractions. You read your Bible and forget what you just read. You thought every time with the Lord was supposed to be fantastic, just like Moses on Mt. Sinai with his 40-day-40-night Ten Commandment party with God. You get up, get some coffee and get ready to have deep, spiritual moments with Him. You know, those quiet times filled with intense, intimate prayer and fascinating scripture reading.

It's not like that in my life. Chances are, it's not like that in yours either.

Sure, you're hanging out with God, and He's probably a Facebook friend and you like His stuff. When asked about your relationship with God, you say, "Fine. Good." But you have no idea. So you read more. Pray more. Give more. Serve more. Share your faith more and wait to grow more spiritually. You dress up for church, smile when you're there and say things like, "God doesn't give you more than you can handle." You try Sunday morning, Sunday night, Wednesday night, a midweek small group. Maybe the answer is hidden in the acoustic worship set or closing prayer or announcements. A-ha. Summer volleyball. You sign up for summer volleyball, dodgeball, basketball, and say things like, "You can do all things through Him." You get in line for the next church program and curriculum, wonder why you're so burned out and think, *God, I hope I don't do something stupid today.*

If spiritual activity and busyness triggered growth, you would be a giant. Instead, you're just tired. You've invested countless hours on spiritual things, and here you are struggling with sin again. The Apostle Paul wrote, "For I do not understand my own actions. For I do not do what I want, but I do the very thing I hate."[2] You try to be good. And fail. You try harder to be good. And fail. Eventually, you don't try so hard, don't live so well, and do what most good Christians do: fake it. You're spiritually stuck. The mess of life gets deeper and dirtier, and stuck is where you are – trying to become more like Christ – but never getting there.

You came to church because of a joy in your heart, excited to be there, but now you show up because you're supposed to. You carry out the same routine, park in the same spot, sit in the same seat, and week after week, it's more of the same. No wonder the church is filled with bored, religious people. There's no grand adventure or higher calling. It's just another Sunday. You keep coming out of a sense of duty with little to show for it, and you're

---

2 Romans 7:15

not growing or maturing in your faith and you're pretty sure it's your own fault.

CHAPTER 2

A MAN ON THE STREET

I THREW OPEN my car door and puked all over the road. I was so desperate to get home that I had snuck out the back of the church. I wanted to be alone, and I was tired but couldn't sleep. Insomnia had taken over. Simple decisions would paralyze me, and I would wake up in the middle of the night wrestling with my thoughts, ideas and to-do's. I was once a thoughtful, decisive leader but now made rash decisions, and the people I was supposed to serve became a bother. Their concerns were overwhelming and their input cut deeply. I would see a familiar face and try not to make eye contact.

I imagined this didn't happen to the spiritual giants I read about in Christian history. They were spending hours in prayer and days fasting for God's will and being humbled. I felt woefully shallow in comparison and humiliated more than anything. I bet their wives parked far enough over so they could fit in the driveway, and their clothes weren't pink, and their keys didn't go missing again. I felt like nothing was good enough, every little thing mattered, and I saw it all. I was running on spiritual vapor and thought, *am I even allowed to struggle? I'm a pastor.*

• • •

YEARS AGO, I gathered a few men I was trying to disciple at a table with one of my spiritual mentors. I had tossed his name around for years, as I owe much of who I am in ministry to this man. I was fired up to see my friends get some time with him as well. We sat in a coffee shop and peppered him with questions. The time passed and it was everything I had hoped for, until one guy asked, "What do you do when you read the Bible and the content feels dry?" You know, the times when you open the scriptures but don't find anything life-changing in the text, or when you are spiritually stuck and the pages just seem to run together.

"Have you felt like that?"

I thought it was a fantastic question and I listened eagerly for the answer. My mentor paused as if recalling some wisdom from deep within, and in a matter-of-fact tone said, "Nope." He got up and left the room. I wasn't sure if I should crawl under the table in shame or call him a liar.

Are you kidding me? Nope. Not one time? You mean to tell me the genealogies of the book of Numbers really spoke to you and the cursing to Edom in Ezekiel was like spiritual fresh air? Great. Then what the heck is wrong with me?

I used to be convinced I was alone in this struggle, but you and I are not much different. It's too easy to say the right things and do the right things because it's what you've always done, and go on living in a spiritual rut with no joy and no life change.

What if God had an entirely different plan for you?

Paul said, "Be imitators of me, as I am of Christ."[3] You're called to be like Him. Your goal is not to become moral, religious, conservative or well behaved, but rather to become more like Jesus. You bear the name Christian as a reminder of your identification with Christ, and He should be what you observe, pursue and emulate.

• • •

3 1 Corinthians 11:1

THERE I WAS PUKING in the street, a pastor puking in the street because this becoming-more-like-Jesus thing is hard and painful. I would rather have you believe I'm a spiritual superman who never struggled and never had a bad day, but my time with the Lord felt stale, isolated and cold. I read, and I was not moved by the words. I served, and it felt like duty. Crazy thing about being a pastor: Sundays just keep coming.

How do I get out of the darkness? How do I lead others out? How can a church follow a man who's still trying to figure it out himself?

I began to live in increased anxiety. I had to teach, I had to deliver, I had to do one more counseling appointment, one more Bible study. It all kept coming. There was no week off or calling in sick, and I pressed on. Sleepless nights killed my energy during the day, so I drank more coffee, and more coffee killed my sleep. I'm an emotional eater, so the diet went out the window for high-sugar treats, fatigue stole the motivation to work out, and just like that, my spiritual collapse was picking up speed. I was pouring my life out to those around me but doing nothing to fill myself back up. The work kept piling on, and I couldn't justify the time for a bike ride or a movie, so I just put my head down and kept going.

I had to get up. What if I don't feel like getting up?

Truth is, I opened my Bible and got nothing out of it, and I tried to pray but was distracted and disconnected. My life was routine, and for some reason, doing the same thing over and over and over led me to the same place. I was desperate to be alone, desperate to work in my yard, sweating in silence, and I found myself hiding from the people I was called to shepherd. I was struggling and most people didn't know. Who could I talk to? It wasn't a crisis of faith; I had a deep and abiding relationship with God. I just didn't feel His presence in my life, and the longer I walked with the Lord, the more pressure I felt to look and act a certain way. I wasn't succeeding at anything important on the inside, so I just overcompensated by succeeding on the outside.

Tired of the insanity, sitting alone and trying to force it, I was going to have to do something different. I couldn't trust my gut because that's what got me stuck in the first place. My college football coach, the legendary Jim Sweeney once said, "If you always do what you have always done, you will always be what you have always been. So if you don't like the way things are going, change the way that you do things."[4]

So I did.

• • •

---

4 Personal translation of Henry Ford

MY FUSE IS SHORT.

There are warning signs of spiritual fatigue, and for me, it's my patience. I'm typically an even-tempered guy, but when stuck happens, I just get picky. It's not anger that begins to surface; it's a critical spirit. The laundry list grows and the criticisms get bigger and more ridiculous, and most of the time, my wife is on the receiving end of ridiculous. It's a vicious cycle and it can show up on a regular basis no matter what I do, and it can be incredibly frustrating. My heart becomes cold and my time in the word is dry.

The scriptures promise the continual presence of God in my life, so I can't blame Him. Maybe I've allowed sin to grow up like a weed, or maybe the very routine meant to kill those weeds is sucking out the spontaneity in my spiritual life. If my wife knows I'm going to spend time with her every morning at 6 a.m., ask the same questions, use the same language, and repeat more of the same, that doesn't do much to inspire depth in our relationship. So why would a routine do so in my relationship with God? My point is, in these times of spiritual loneliness, I realize it's not Him; it's me.

So while stuck still comes, and while sometimes I stay there longer than others, I have learned getting out usually starts like this, more or less: confess utter helplessness, humble myself and ask the Lord to give me strength, develop better self-awareness to recognize the signs of spiritual decline earlier, figure out what fills me up and do those things, and finally, invite people in to help me out.

> Jesus said…"Everyone who drinks of this water will be thirsty again, but whoever drinks of the water that I will give him will never be thirsty again. The water that I will give him will become in him a spring of water welling up to eternal life."[5]

He has promised refreshment and fulfillment to those who follow Him. He's calling us out of the darkness, and yet I've watched good, God-loving people just quit, and while they may never admit it, have resigned to enjoy heaven and fake it until then.

You can follow things in this world that promise you everything and deliver nothing. You can look to your career, relationships, influence or affluence, or look to the one who laid down His life for you and took it up again. No one will deliver fulfillment or peace or justice or equality like Jesus Christ. Do you profess faith in Him and still live like you don't know better? If you love Him, do what He says. Are you paying attention? He's always speaking to you and you must continue to answer Him.

---

5 John 4:13-14

CHAPTER 3

CADENCE OF THE OARSMAN

MY PARENTS DIVORCED when I was nine, and my dad knew leaving me home alone with my brother after school was going to be trouble. So he thought it would be a good idea to get me into as many extra-curricular activities as possible. I played baseball and soccer and football, ran cross-country and track, and wrestled. I was on a wrestling mat by third grade, and to be honest, I was on my back most of the time. By junior high I knew the number of lights in almost every gym in our city, but I kept at it. It was senior year when my wrestling career blossomed, and I finished the season with 53 wins and one loss to a guy named Zach Cooper.

Wrestling tournaments are some of the loudest events you can imagine. The larger tournaments were three-day events depending on the number of schools invited, and there could be eight matches happening at one time. It was a cacophony of sound with literally everyone and their mother yelling: coaches screaming at the referees, teammates calling out moves, whistles, horns, cheerleaders, and parents throwing in their two cents. The voices filled the room, and as I fatigued on the mat, it became more difficult to differentiate between them. Was that my coach or a guy ordering a hot dog?

However, there was one voice I could always hear. My dad. He wasn't a coach, though he yelled like one, and weekend after weekend, match after match, he was there. Yelling. It was as if there was a distinction to his voice, as if something deep within me could distinctly hear it and recognize it was his. When he spoke, it was not just another voice, and when he called, I heard him.

In John, Jesus says, "I am the good shepherd. I know my own and my own know me, just as the Father knows me and I know the Father; and I lay down my life for the sheep."[6] Jesus continues, "My sheep hear my voice, and I know them, and they follow me."[7] My dad wasn't a shepherd; he was a car salesman. Though when I read this passage, it all made sense. I have heard my dad's voice so often it has become familiar, and that familiarity has given his voice precedence over competing voices. I have

---

6 John 10:14-15
7 John 10:27

learned over time to pick his voice out of a crowd. I knew he was there, and I was listening for it, anticipating it, and in many ways, longing for it. If I was beginning a wrestling match, he might yell for me to shoot, which would award two points for a takedown. If I was in a good position, he might yell for me to do a specific move. He pointed out things I couldn't see and called for me to act.

Can you recognize God's voice? It's not an audible voice but more of a gentle stirring in your soul. The Bible tells you, "None is righteous, no, not one; no one understands; no one seeks for God."[8] If you ever begin to see something of concern in your spiritual life, ever come to a greater spiritual understanding, if you're ever stirred to address something spiritually, or ever long to be more like Jesus in some way – that is the voice of God. Can you hear Him? He's already at work in your life telling you what to do, and while this world can drown Him out amidst the busyness, you must hear what He has to say. "Jesus Christ is the same yesterday and today and forever."[9] He's still your "Good Shepherd" calling you out of the darkness even today.

Again, God is already at work in you, so what's your role in becoming more like Jesus? He calls and you respond. He calls and you respond. He calls and you respond.

• • •

---

8 Romans 3:10-11
9 Hebrews 13:8

IN HAWAII, a group of locals well into their fifties challenged myself and some others to a canoe race. Being the strong and fit, thirty-somethings we were, the advantage should have been ours. They had a head oarsman who called out the cadence, and they paddled. He called; they paddled. It seemed as if their boat literally came out of the water, and skimming the top, began to fly. As they pulled away, we exerted more and more effort but never paddled to the cadence of the oarsman.

The spiritual life works in a similar partnership. When you hear God call, you must respond or you will not move. Likewise, if you exert effort but are not listening for the call, your effort will be fruitless.

So is spiritual growth your responsibility or does God drive the process? The answer is yes.

The book of Acts chronicles the early church as the gospel was moving rapidly and the message of the resurrected Savior was being well received outside of Jerusalem. Paul began to pioneer church plants in Galatia, Macedonia and Achaia (modern-day Turkey and Greece), and these new churches had difficulty reconciling the law of Judaism and this new freedom in Christ. They assumed salvation was by faith alone, by grace alone, in Christ alone, and then – you were on your own. Paul said, "Let me ask you only this: Did you receive the Spirit by works of the law or by hearing with faith? Are you so foolish? Having begun by the Spirit, are you now being perfected by the flesh?"[10]

They faced the same perceived theological contradictions Christians have been arguing over for centuries. For example, did you choose God or did God choose you? The answer is yes. At a moment in time you chose God, yet in that very moment God orchestrated the circumstances in your life, which brought you to that decision. The Bible communicates both realities and doesn't apologize for what would seem to be a contradiction.

I will ask again: is spiritual growth your responsibility or does God drive the process? Yes. Paul told the church in the city of Philippi, "Therefore, my beloved, as you have always obeyed, so now, not only as in my presence but much more in my absence, work out your own salvation with fear and trembling, for it is God who works in you, both to will and to work for his good pleasure."[11] Work on your own salvation with fear and trembling, which means invest time in it, be aware of it and allow it to be a priority in your life. That is your responsibility, and you will not grow in Christ if you sit back and do nothing, waiting for God to move you closer to Him. However, the rest of the passage points to God working in your life for His good pleasure. In other words, God initiates any and all spiritual growth.

---

10 Galatians 3:2-3
11 Philippians 2:12–13

En route to the Garden of Gethsemane on the night He was betrayed, Jesus said, "Abide in me, and I in you. As the branch cannot bear fruit by itself, unless it abides in the vine, neither can you, unless you abide in me. I am the vine; you are the branches. Whoever abides in me and I in him, he it is that bears much fruit, for apart from me you can do nothing."[12] It all starts with Him. He is the source.

Unfortunately, many spiritual formation plans and programs fail to communicate both sides, focusing very little on God's initiative and more so on human responsibility, which assumes if you're growing spiritually, you possess self-discipline and determination. On the other hand, if you're not growing spiritually, then you're weak and worldly.

You can muster up the courage to be more disciplined, to modify or abstain from certain behaviors by your own determination for a little while. Human effort alone will never bring about spiritual growth, yet you have been pointed to exactly that. You're taught to fast, have quiet times, block inappropriate digital content and join accountability groups. You've put external boundaries on life to help you make good decisions: don't drink alcohol, don't dance, don't listen to music. Paul says, "Do not handle, Do not taste, Do not touch."[13] But he continues, "These have indeed an appearance of wisdom in promoting self-made religion and asceticism and

---

12 John 15:4-5
13 Colossians 2:21

severity to the body, but they are of no value in stopping the indulgence of the flesh."[14] Do you see that? These moral boundaries are meaningless in stopping the indulgence of the flesh.

You will not grow in Christ if you blaze your own trail. I think of it in terms of following His lead. He initiates but you must follow. He stirs and you move. If you do, if you begin to follow the Good Shepherd, you will begin to look like the Good Shepherd.

---

14 Colossians 2:23

CHAPTER 4

INSIDE OUT

GOD IS ALWAYS MESSING with you, every part of you, chipping away at your heart, your mind, your choices and your compassions. Crazy thing though, He hasn't left you to figure it out on your own, for "he who began a good work in you will bring it to completion at the day of Jesus Christ."[15] He has promised to help you become more like Jesus and He will finish it.

A sculptor chips away, intimately aware of the movement of sediment, of the curves, lines and coloration within a stone. Instead of creating from nothing, he begins with something and removes what doesn't belong, one tiny piece at a time, until all that remains is what was in the stone to begin with.

---

15 Philippians 1:6

God is a sculptor. He sees His image in you and is patiently chipping away, one tiny imperfection at a time, the things that are not like Him, and He's starting in your heart.

The spiritual life is broken down into four key areas (shown here as concentric rings): heart, mind, choices and compassions.

Authentic spiritual growth is going to move from your very core outward, beginning in the center and slowly spilling over into the outer rings of your life. If you want to intentionally become more like Jesus, it's not you who lives; it's Christ who lives in you.

You need to have a heart for God.

At the core of your spiritual life is your heart and He's fighting for it. Why? "As in water face reflects face, so the heart of man reflects the man."[16] It's the real you, the root of all emotion, the beginning of all action, and the source of what your life produces, and that's why you're called by God to guard it diligently. "Keep your heart with all vigilance, for from it flow the springs of life."[17] God knows that everything you do starts with the heart, and He's in a battle for your affections: what you value, what's important

16 Proverbs 27:19
17 Proverbs 4:23

and what moves you, all things that come from the heart. Proverbs tells you to "keep my commandments and live; keep my teaching as the apple of your eye; bind them on your fingers; write them on the tablet of your heart."[18]

The very center of it all is what God is doing in your heart, but then it's going to move. The way you live is impacted by the affections of your heart and then by what you think.

You need to have a mind formed by His word.

While your heart provides the motivation, your mind is how you understand life: what you believe, how you reason, and ultimately how you act on it. "Do not be conformed to this world, but be transformed by the renewal of your mind, that by testing you may discern what is the will of God, what is good and acceptable and perfect."[19] Your mind, filtered through His word, sorts through the barrage of messages you hear, helping you decide what is truth and what is foolishness.

Authentic spiritual growth is going to move from your heart to your mind until it spills out into every area of your life: areas of generosity, areas of morality and areas of relationship. What God is doing inside you, at your very core, is going to move outward and begin to affect what you do, how you do it and why you do it.

---

18 Proverbs 7:2-3
19 Romans 12:2

As God changes your heart and mind, your choices will begin to point toward Him.

You're called by God to reflect His image in the world around you. "You are the salt of the earth, but if salt has lost its taste, how shall its saltiness be restored? It is no longer good for anything except to be thrown out and trampled under people's feet."[20] Your faith is intended to be lived out loud, and your choices seen on the outside say everything about who you are on the inside. Do you confess faith in Christ? Have you allowed Him to shape your mind? If so, then your actions will follow. "By this we may know that we are in him: whoever says he abides in him ought to walk in the same way in which he walked."[21] If your actions don't reveal His character, the problem is not merely your behavior but something much deeper, for the choices you make reflect your heart and mind.

When you have a heart for God and your mind is filtered through His word, your choices will be affected, and that will mess with your compassions.

The biblical word used for compassion carries with it the powerful idea of experiencing great affection with action. Meaning more than feeling bad for someone, it's being deeply moved and compelled to respond. A private, contained, unmoved spiritual life

---

20 Matthew 5:13
21 1 John 2:5-6

is a broken spiritual life. If you're not stirred to action by injustice or moved with passion in some way, then there's a much deeper problem. The answer is not to serve the poor or feed the homeless, but rather to submit your heart to God and read His word, for only then will you be compelled to live differently. And He's preparing a place for you to serve Him right now. Paul said, "For we are his workmanship, created in Christ Jesus for good works, which God prepared beforehand, that we should walk in them."[22] God will eventually awaken an area of compassion in you that He has specifically prepared for you. Again, God is chipping away at your heart, mind, choices and compassions, exposing things unique to you and stirring you to action.

Authentic spiritual growth is going to begin in your heart and mind, and it's going to work its way out into the way you live. The spiritual life is not for you alone. The whole point is that your life would reflect Christ to the world around you as you look more and more like Jesus.

Great. So what does Jesus actually look like? Better yet, how do you know whether or not you're actively becoming more like Him?

• • •

---

22 Ephesians 2:10

31

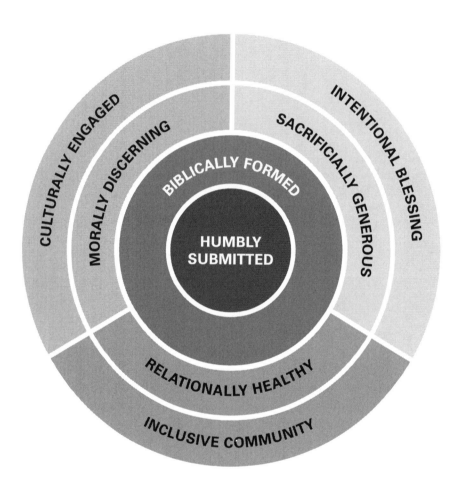

THE ANATOMY of a Disciple is the guts, the insides, of what a mature follower of Christ looks like. The life of Jesus was complicated, but when I look at Him, I can identify at least eight elements. These are the things Jesus was about, who He was and how He lived, and these are traits you should be aware of as you intentionally pursue Him.

Humbly Submitted
Biblically Formed
Sacrificially Generous
Intentional Blessing
Morally Discerning
Culturally Engaged
Relationally Healthy
Inclusive Community

The four concentric rings of authentic spiritual growth are further broken down into these eight elements. What makes The Anatomy of a Disciple so unique is the intentional movement from the inside out, from one individual element to the other. The elements don't stand alone or act as a checklist, but are intimately connected to each other and work together.

As a disciple of Christ, you must have a heart that's Humbly Submitted to God and a mind that's Biblically Formed before life change can happen in areas of generosity, relationship and morality. If you say, *God, I have a heart for you, and I love you, and I want to see what the Bible says about whatever,* now you're doing life differently as a result. So hang on and enjoy the ride.

Is God the most important thing in your life? Yes.

How are you doing spiritually? Fine. Good.

How do you know? Do you have an objective way of explaining how you're doing, or are you just guessing? Your husband isn't that angry with you this week. You haven't looked at that much porn. Your church attendance is up. You gave the guy at the corner a couple bucks. All these things are superficial, and *fine* and *good* are woefully vague. You need to take a good, hard, honest look at where you are growing and are not growing spiritually.

Put down the book and go to **anatomyofadisciple.com**. The Anatomy of a Disciple self-assessment takes you through the eight elements, helping you see, objectively and with clarity, how you're really doing spiritually.

As I define each element in the following chapters, use your self-assessment results to help you see where God is already at work in your life. You will see things unique to you, things that are not in alignment with the life of Christ, and things He wants you to work on. Ask God, *what are you doing?* The key to this whole process is awareness. The elements will show themselves again and again in your life, and He will use them to help you hear His voice. He will use them to make you more like Jesus, so prayerfully ask God to finish what He started.

CHAPTER 5

HUMBLY SUBMITTED

DEFIANCE IS GENETIC. Seconds removed from a mother's womb, children make their first statement to the world, and typically in the form of a scream, they're letting you know they're not happy. Over time, the screams become tones, and tones soon gather into syllables. Then one day they're armed with words and the demands become more sophisticated, yet carry the same primal roots of defiance. Children believe the world revolves around them and they are of central importance, and they assume everyone else agrees with this.

There are books on raising boys, cultivating inner beauty in girls, surviving a blended family, single parenting, and everything in between. However, you will never find a book on how to train your child to be selfish or a book titled "How To Teach Your Child To Say No." Why? They don't need any training to hone these skills. They come about them quite naturally.

There's a little aspiring narcissist in all of us, and while you may have more sophisticated language skills, the tantrums are just as disturbing. When the world revolves around you, life is good. When it doesn't, you protest. You like playing God, and at the center of it all is the continued desire to be in control, to have power and to live according to your preferences. Something deep down inside is broken from birth. So where did these character faults originate?

What was the first sin in the Bible? Most people would turn to Genesis 3 and note the fall of mankind, but the first sin happened before that, at least chronologically. Isaiah 14 and Ezekiel 28 record the fall of Satan. Satan was a chief angel created by God with special privilege and authority, and despite his esteemed position, he wanted to be in charge. Isaiah 14 records seven "I will" statements he makes in defiance of God. Satan wanted to be God, and in the end, that didn't work out so well. He was ejected from the presence of God and sent to the earth with one-third of the angelic realm that had joined his rebellion. What was the nature of his offense? Pride.

In Genesis, pride assaults mankind in the Garden of Eden.

Adam and Eve are ruling over creation and enjoying the commands of God to be fruitful, multiply, fill the earth and subdue it. That is, until Satan shows up. He begins to expose Eve's deep-rooted desire to be in control by saying, "For God knows that when you eat of it your eyes will be opened, and you will be like God, knowing good and evil."[23] Satan convinces Eve if God were really good, He would share this wonderful insight with her. He deceives her into thinking God doesn't want what's best for her, and in fact, is holding out, and she could be like Him, calling the shots. "So when the woman saw that the tree was good for food, and that it was a delight to the eyes, and that the tree was to be desired to make one wise, she took of its fruit and ate, and she also gave some to her husband who was with her, and he ate."[24]

The fall of Adam and Eve is why all of mankind is born with a natural bent toward sin. You are born with a desire to be prideful, and God is not a fan.

"God opposes the proud, but gives grace to the humble."[25]

God stands in opposition of a pride-filled life, and pride is a sneaky little beast. How do you know when you're prideful? When you care too much about what people think of you. Pride. When you care too much about what you drive, how you dress or where

---

23 Genesis 3:5
24 Genesis 3:6
25 James 4:6

you live. Pride. When you use sarcasm to put people down. Pride. When jealousy creeps in, when you grasp for accolades, when you grasp for power, position or influence. Pride.

Pride is relentless and can cause a slow and subtle drift away from God, and you must be vigilant in your resistance.

> Humble yourselves, therefore, under the mighty hand of God so that at the proper time he may exalt you, casting all your anxieties on him, because he cares for you. Be sober-minded; be watchful. Your adversary the devil prowls around like a roaring lion, seeking someone to devour. Resist him, firm in your faith, knowing that the same kinds of suffering are being experienced by your brotherhood throughout the world.[26]

When I was a kid, like most, I tested my dad's patience, and it often involved pushing boundaries, toying with consequences, and ultimately calling down paternal wrath upon myself. I can remember when I had done something stupid, my dad would say, "There are two ways that we can go about this: the easy way and the hard way. The choice is yours." As I read the passage above, I hear my dad's voice. You can humble yourself or you can be humbled, and the choice is yours.

---

26 1 Peter 5:6-9

You're a modern-day narcissist, born in sin, living in immorality, overflowing with pride and expressing a profound commitment to self. I hate to break it to you, but you're not always right, your ideas are not always the best, you're not always the most popular, and when it comes to the things of God, you're not in control. He is.

So can you trust God? Can He be counted on? Does He have your best interests at heart?

Humility is never easy, and let's be honest, you don't enjoy relinquishing control. However, you're not submitting to an earthly authority but to the God of the universe. His ways are good, holy and just. Always. He is consistent and faithful, and His love is enduring. Always. The sooner you become Humbly Submitted to God, the sooner authentic spiritual growth can happen.

• • •

HAVE YOU EVER been around someone who thought they were a really big deal? Several years ago, I was traveling with my bride en route to Africa for a mission trip. After an excruciatingly long flight, we landed in London. We happened to be on the airplane with a very high-profile celebrity, who deplaned in style, her hair perfectly done and dressed in the highest fashion, with entourage in tow. The crowds began to assemble, but before the chaos fully erupted, she took a quick stop in the loo. My wife, who had also stopped in to freshen up, shared a mirror with this woman. Amidst the noise of flushing toilets and howling hand dryers, she was reminded that people who think they're a big deal still use the loo like the rest of us.

If there was ever someone who deserved fanfare, it was Jesus, the Savior and Lord incarnating into this world. Yet there was no grand entrance or paparazzi, just the splayed legs of a teenage girl in a manger. There was no party, just some shepherds and a few farm animals, and there were few gifts, three to be exact, brought from afar by three kings from the East. Jesus, deity clothed in humanity, entered the world and most didn't even notice.

Jesus didn't grasp for power, prestige or control. In fact, he emptied Himself and became a servant in the likeness of men.

Have this mind among yourselves, which is yours in Christ Jesus, who, though he was in the form of God, did not count equality with God a thing to be grasped, but emptied himself, by taking the form of a servant, being born in the likeness of men. And being found in human form, he humbled himself by becoming obedient to the point of death, even death on a cross.[27]

In the shadow of the cross, just hours before His crucifixion, Jesus prayed in hope for an alternative.

"Father, if you are willing, remove this cup from me. Nevertheless, not my will, but yours, be done."[28]

The message of Jesus was not about becoming impressive but rather becoming a servant. From birth to execution, Jesus didn't claim special privilege or flex His rights, He was not swayed by pride, but personified humility, and He enjoyed a simple life with the common man.

Jesus said, "Blessed are the poor in spirit, for theirs is the kingdom of heaven. Blessed are those who mourn, for they shall be comforted. Blessed are the meek, for they shall inherit the earth. Blessed are those who hunger and thirst for righteousness, for they shall be satisfied."[29]

---

27 Philippians 2:5-8
28 Luke 22:42
29 Matthew 5:3-6

If you're "poor in spirit," you recognize the depth of your pride, realizing you're broken at the core of who you are. You're poor or bankrupt in your own spirit and spiritual abilities, and you know it, and having seen the futility of a self-centered life, you now embrace the fact you're not in control.

If you're "those who mourn," you admit how stained or wrecked you are by sin in your life, and having seen the depth of your selfishness, you have turned to God through brokenness.

If you're "the meek," you don't insist on having your own way. Exhausted from years of trying to fight God, you have recognized the futility of your efforts, have relinquished control, and have given your life over to another authority.

These three traits are present if you have progressively come to the end of yourself.

Jesus continues, "Blessed are those who hunger and thirst for righteousness, for they shall be satisfied." In this context, the words hunger and thirst are descriptions of desperation, meaning you have an intense longing for righteousness and ultimately find satisfaction in this pursuit.

• • •

I'M SOMEWHAT OF a hobby junkie, and about every two years I need a new fix in an obsessive, all-or-nothing kind of way. Change energizes me and constantly picking up something new keeps me learning. First it was coffee, then cycling, firearms, CrossFit, endurance races and gardening. I blame my Israeli friend Ronen for that last one. I was leading a tour in Israel and Ronen was talking about the heart of the Jewish people to cultivate the land. I was intrigued by the concept and noticed all of the abundance being grown in Israel: fruit trees, nuts, berries, vines, bananas and dates. It was indeed the land flowing with milk and honey, and I thought about my home and my sorry excuse for a backyard. All summer long I would fight to keep the grass from dying in the heat. What if I ripped out my lawn and planted some food?

So I planted 15 fruit trees (mandarin orange, peach, cherry, nectarine, kumquat, pomegranate, fig, lemon, orange and pluot), 13 grapevines, 6 raspberry, 4 blueberry and 2 blackberry bushes, and more than 200-square-feet of raised vegetable beds. I admit it's a bit excessive, but again, all or nothing. It has been an agricultural adventure that brought my wife and two girls together for hours, and as with any great experiment, there's a steep learning curve. We are learning about planting, pruning, harvesting, composting, integrated pest management and weeds. My girls enjoy watching things grow, and I love to see their excitement as something begins to sprout.

Unfortunately, most of what we see sprouting are weeds. "Daddy, is that a carrot?" they ask. "Nope, that's a weed," I reply. "Daddy, is that broccoli?" they ask. "Nope, that's a weed," I say with a sigh. It's as if the weeds have come up overnight. One day they're not there, and the next they have mocked me yet again. Pulling weeds is a regular part of managing a garden, and it's not a matter of if weeds will grow, it's about how many and how we'll deal with them. So we have committed to examine our garden weekly and pull the weeds before they take over.

Pride is a weed in your spiritual life, and God is constantly revealing these weeds before they take over. There are moments when you are made aware of the pride in your life, which may seem docile at the time, but if left unchecked, the consequences can be devastating.

> I passed by the field of a sluggard, by the vineyard of a man lacking sense, and behold, it was all overgrown with thorns; the ground was covered with nettles, and its stone wall was broken down. Then I saw and considered it; I looked and received instruction. A little sleep, a little slumber, a little folding of the hands to rest, and poverty will come upon you like a robber, and want like an armed man.[30]

The cause of this devastation was not a spontaneous event, but rather the accumulation of small things over time. It was a little

---

30 Proverbs 24:30-34

sleep, a little slumber and a little folding of the hands to rest, and it's the little allowances of sin in your life that lead to chaos.

My girls point at something, not sure if it's a weed or not, and listen for my voice. If I tell them it's a weed, they pull it out. So what is God showing you? Are there areas of your life where self is still trying to be in control? If you're not sure, ask Him. God longs for you to become more like Jesus, and He is at work to accomplish that very purpose. However, the process of spiritual growth requires constant watch as He points out the weeds that need your attention. So make sure you're living Humbly Submitted to God in every area of your life. He emptied Himself and became a servant, and He calls you to do the same.

You want to matter, but while you're busy thinking of yourself and grasping to be seen, He can never increase. You must become aware of what God is doing in your life, then get out of His way and get on board with it. You must decrease for Him to increase. That's how it works. Until you do, until you realize He's more important than you, He will never increase, and if He never increases, you will always be spiritually stagnant.

WHERE DO YOU GO FROM HERE?

Here are some steps you can take to begin to grow more Humbly Submitted to God:

PRAYER

Search me, O God, and know my heart! Try me and know my thoughts! And see if there be any grievous way in me, and lead me in the way everlasting![31]

Be prepared. If you pray like this, God will answer. God is at work in your life, and He's pointing out the weeds of pride, anger, selfishness, arrogance, competition, comparison and jealousy. He never tires of exposing the last strongholds of self you're holding onto. Jesus said, "If anyone wishes to come after Me, he must deny himself, and take up his cross and follow Me."[32] As God begins to reveal these things, take the time to prayerfully repent of the sin of pride that has grown in your life.

SIMPLE SELF-EVALUATION

You know your heart. Have you been angry recently? If so, why? Have you been jealous or sarcastic? What does God bring to mind? The process of self-examination teaches you to be aware of the weeds in your garden, and God is constantly pointing things

---

31 Psalm 139:23-24
32 Mark 8:34, NASB

out to you. Sometimes it's a gentle nudge, and other times it's a bit more forceful, but He's always working. He's constantly opening your eyes to that which you did not see at first.

ASK, "WHAT DO YOU SEE?"

Sometimes you don't see yourself as clearly as others do. If someone in your life loves you enough to be candid, ask, "What do you see? What sin issues do you see in me? Do you see pride in me? If so, when?"

If you are married, this can be a fantastic conversation with your spouse. These questions bring about good, honest dialogue and can deepen a marriage quickly. However, the truth can hurt. You can hide sin from the world, but a spouse can see through the ruse and call out sins you're either denying or have grown so accustomed to they have become the normal in your life.

LEARN REPENTANCE AND RESTORATION

When you find pride in your life, quickly turn to God and ask for forgiveness, placing yourself under His authority. Remember, God is opposed to the proud, and this means He takes on pride viciously. Repentance is the act of recognizing the direction you are heading and turning the other way. It's also good to be reminded that when you repent, "he is faithful and just to forgive us our sins and to cleanse us from all unrighteousness."[33]

Restoration comes when you seek to repair relationship with those you have wounded with your pride. Though you receive forgiveness from God through prayer, restoration requires you to also follow up with those you've hurt. Ask their forgiveness. A sincere "I'm sorry" is a very simple but powerful phrase.

---

[33] 1 John 1:9

CHAPTER 6

BIBLICALLY FORMED

A FAITHFUL SECOND in command, Joshua is a stout warrior charged with leading God's people after the death of Moses. In the first chapter of the book of Joshua, God encourages him to be "strong and courageous" four different times.[34] Why? He was terrified. Of all the biblical characters to follow, how would you like to come after Moses? Moses: the exodus from Egypt, the plagues and the Red Sea. Those are some serious shoes to fill, and Joshua needed to know how to be a strong leader as his fear and insecurity had begun to creep in.

> This Book of the Law shall not depart from your mouth,
> but you shall meditate on it day and night, so that you may

---

34 See Joshua 1:6, 7, 9, 18

be careful to do according to all that is written in it. For then you will make your way prosperous, and then you will have good success.[35]

Joshua was called to keep the law of God ever before him, and he was to spend time in the text, to read it, learn from it, study it and talk about it often. That's what meditate means in this context. Joshua was to always be muttering the word of God, his mouth filled with the word of God all day, every day, and even his thoughts were to be about the text. However, it wasn't knowledge alone that would lead him to success and prosperity, and it wasn't enough to merely regurgitate quotations from the Bible. Joshua had to do what the text said and obey what he was reading. As Joshua meditated on the word and applied what he was thinking about, he would be transformed into the type of leader God created him to be. His success would be based upon his obedience to the text and not on his charisma or strength. His prosperity would be defined by God's standards and not his own.

And Joshua the son of Nun, the servant of the LORD, died at the age of 110 years. And they buried him within the boundaries of his inheritance in Timnath-heres, in the hill country of Ephraim, north of the mountain of Gaash. And all that generation also were gathered to their fathers. And there arose another generation after them who did not

---

35 Joshua 1:8

know the LORD or the work that he had done for Israel.[36]

The entire book of Judges records what happens when people drift away from the knowledge of, and obedience to, the text. The chaotic downward spiral culminates in chapters 17-21, bookended with the same phrase: "In those days there was no king in Israel. Everyone did what was right in his own eyes."[37] Sounds liberating, right? Bound by no rules, they determined what worked best for them.

They rejected the word of God, as did Adam and Eve in the very beginning. Eve trusted her own finite sense of reason, doing what she thought was right. She saw the tree was good for food, and seduced by its beauty, assumed it would make her wise, so she ate. Satan promised she would be like God, but instead she was ejected from the Garden, separated from God, distanced from her husband, and she cursed the entire creation for all time because of her disobedience.

Are you seduced by what looks good? Truthfully, not much has changed since the Garden of Eden.

Do not love the world or the things in the world. If anyone loves the world, the love of the Father is not in him. For all that is in the world – the desires of the flesh and the desires

36 Judges 2:8-10
37 Judges 17:6; 21:25

of the eyes and pride of life – is not from the Father but is from the world.[38]

The gravitational pull of the world is away from the things of God. Our flesh doesn't celebrate godliness, rather finds itself drawn to another cocktail, the desire to accumulate more, an emotional connection to someone outside of marriage. The desires of your flesh and your eyes and your pride do not originate from God but from the world, and the text helps you determine what is of God and what is not.

I appeal to you therefore, brothers, by the mercies of God, to present your bodies as a living sacrifice, holy and acceptable to God, which is your spiritual worship. Do not be conformed to this world, but be transformed by the renewal of your mind, that by testing you may discern what is the will of God, what is good and acceptable and perfect.[39]

Paul understood the church in Rome would struggle in its daily battle of living for Christ, and his words are just as relevant today. Notice the progression: since God has already done all of this for you, how should you then respond to Him? You should offer yourself to Him as someone who is Humbly Submitted to His rule and authority in your life, daily. Don't be conformed to the

---

38 1 John 2:15-16
39 Romans 12:1-2

world, but instead be transformed by the renewing of your mind. In this context, conformed means to be shoved into a mold, and without the text, the world sets the standard and you're made to look like those around you. Without the word of God shaping the way you think, morality becomes an issue of opinion.

You must live a life of obedience to God and not of personal preference, which by the way, is completely unnatural. What does perfect obedience to the scriptures even look like in real life?

• • •

I WAS COMPLETELY LOST. Before I placed my faith in Christ, I was encouraged to read the Gospel of John, and within the first five verses, was so confused.

> In the beginning was the Word, and the Word was with God, and the Word was God. He was in the beginning with God. All things were made through him, and without him was not any thing made that was made. In him was life, and the life was the light of men. The light shines in the darkness, and the darkness has not overcome it.[40]

In the beginning was the Word? The Word was with God? The Word was God?

It wasn't until years later that I began to realize the significance of this passage. The first several verses speak of the Word, and notice it's capitalized. The word literally carries the idea of a verbal echo of all that is God, and the author is starting his Gospel by clearly identifying Jesus as the perfect representation of all that is God. He is the Word. The deity of Christ is indicated again when John says, "And the Word became flesh and dwelt among us, and we have seen his glory, glory as of the only Son from the Father, full of grace and truth."[41] In other words, he's saying Jesus, the perfect embodiment of God in human flesh, dwelt among them and they saw Him up close and personal, and it was fantastic.

---

40 John 1:1-5
41 John 1:14

Some thought He had come to set aside the Law or the Prophets, but on the contrary, He had come to fulfill them.[42] Even as a twelve-year-old boy, His knowledge and application of the text had stumped the scholars of His day, "And all who heard him were amazed at his understanding and his answers."[43] His entire life, every thought and deed, was lived in perfect obedience. Never a lustful thought, never a word spoken in anger, never a disobedient action. Not one.

Fatigued and hungry, Jesus was tempted by Satan in the Judean wilderness for forty days and forty nights. Satan used three specific temptations designed to woo Him away from obedience to the word: an invitation to power, relevance and abundance. Jesus responded to each one, "It is written,"[44] and proceeded to quote the book of Deuteronomy. In time of greatest weakness, the text was His strength.

> For I did not speak on My own initiative, but the Father Himself who sent Me has given Me a commandment *as to* what to say and what to speak. I know that His commandment is eternal life; therefore the things I speak, I speak just as the Father has told Me.[45]

Jesus relied on the word of God and adjusted His decisions

---

42 See Matthew 5:17
43 Luke 2:47
44 See Matthew 4
45 John 12:49-50, NASB

and actions into complete alignment with the will of the Father, and He wants the same from you. He said, "Whoever has my commandments and keeps them, he it is who loves me."[46] God expected that those who claim to love Jesus would obey the Scriptures.

John put it this way: "Whoever says 'I know him' but does not keep his commandments is a liar, and the truth is not in him."[47] Those are strong words, but if you're to become more and more like the person of Christ, you must allow the word of God to transform your mind to be more like His.

• • •

46 John 14:21
47 1 John 2:4

YOU'RE BORED IN your spiritual life because you don't read the book. When you read the word of God, the word of God will mess with your life. Sometimes you're going to close the book and think, *okay?* Sometimes you're going to close the book and think, *whoa, that was for me. How did He know I needed that?*

Take your Bible and read it, and I don't mean like you read a novel once, way back when. I mean do you read it? Like today, did you read it? How about tomorrow, will you read it then? How about the next day? Read just a little bit every day depending on how much time you've got. Maybe it's a chapter. Try it for a year, or maybe four days. See what happens.

The same Spirit of God that fills you as a believer is the same Spirit of God that inspired the text. So trust that when you read it, He's going to show you something or do something in you.

All scripture is breathed out by God and profitable for teaching, for reproof, for correction, and for training in righteousness, that the man of God may be complete, equipped for every good work.[48]

Teaching – You will see the truths or paths of life God has designed for you. The word of God becomes the authoritative source of right and wrong, and your life is brought into alignment with Him.

48 2 Timothy 3:16-17

61

Reproof – God uses His word to bring you back to Him. Think of reproof as the gentle voice of a GPS unit recalculating when you make a wrong turn. It won't get angry or raise its voice, it simply provides an alert you're blazing your own trail. The word of God will clearly show you when you're off course and gently nudge you back.

Correction – You will be brought into alignment with His truth, and not by way of subtle suggestion. The word of God will directly confront your worldly thinking, using specific text to expose your carnal or fleshly needs, and then bring you back into alignment with Him once more.

Training in Righteousness – The word of God will provide instruction, and over time, train you in righteousness or proper habits of behavior. Lessons are learned slowly and, at times, through brokenness. Spiritual maturity is not an easy process or a quick one.

I think of my time in the word like eating a meal. I can't tell you what I had for lunch last Tuesday, but I can tell you about the filet I had for dinner. Both meals were nourishing, but only one was memorable. What happens when you read the Bible and forget what you read? Does it lose its value? Does my lunch only nourish my body if I remember it? Of course not. The point is to eat anyway.

You come to church to get fed, and then leave your Bible in the car so you don't forget it next week. You're waiting for just another Sunday, and while you wait, you can't figure out why you keep looking at pornography, keep crossing the line with your girlfriend or boyfriend, and are disrespectful to your parents.

Paul said, "Yet if it had not been for the law, I would not have known sin. For I would not have known what it is to covet if the law had not said, 'You shall not covet.'"[49]

After I placed my faith in Christ, I got serious about my time in the word. Like Paul, I was made aware of the sin issues in my life, and page after page the text revealed things that were out of alignment with who God is. My sin list was long and growing daily, and the more I read, the more I was made aware. I read: "Let no unwholesome word proceed from your mouth, but only such *a word* as is good for edification according to the need *of the moment,* so that it will give grace to those who hear."[50] I immediately realized I needed to stop cussing. I read: "And do not get drunk with wine, for that is dissipation, but be filled with the Spirit,"[51] and realized I needed to deal with my drinking. I read: "For this is the will of God, your sanctification: that you abstain from sexual immorality; that each one of you know how to control his own body in holiness and honor, not in the passion of lust like the Gentiles who do

---

49 Romans 7:7
50 Ephesians 4:29, NASB
51 Ephesians 5:18, NASB

not know God,"[52] and realized I needed to keep my zipper up. I thought, *God, I'm a mess.* He answered, *I know, but now you're being honest. So let's grow.*

The word of God will get in your face, never relent, never let you off the hook, and has the power to change your life, even today. When you read it and do what it says – when you treat a woman in a way that honors Christ, when you don't get tipsy at a party, when you take unwholesome words and thoughts captive – now you're pursuing Jesus.

In the book of Nehemiah, a copy of the Bible was found in the rubble in Jerusalem. They built a wooden platform and gave the scrolls to Ezra, a young scribe, to read out loud to the entire city. The text says he would read a portion of the scripture and then let some of his colleagues walk through the crowd answering any questions. Then, he would keep reading. "For Ezra had set his heart to study the Law of the Lord, and to do it and to teach his statutes and rules in Israel."[53] He read the word of God from early morning until midday and the people stood in ovation. What a sight that must have been! Have you ever known someone who was great at eloquently waxing scripture but not so great at living it? Not Ezra. He set his heart to read, to dig into the text, to learn what it said, and then, to practice what he was learning in his own life.

---

52 1 Thessalonians 4:3-5
53 Ezra 7:10

God is at work helping you become more Biblically Formed, and your time in the word will begin to reveal issues He wants you to work on. While the issues may seem never-ending, God will faithfully bring to mind the things He wants you to deal with, when He wants you to deal with them.

> For the word of God is living and active, sharper than any two-edged sword, piercing to the division of soul and of spirit, of joints and of marrow, and discerning the thoughts and intentions of the heart. And no creature is hidden from his sight, but all are naked and exposed to the eyes of him to whom we must give account.[54]

The word of God will wreck you, and it will expose where you're not living right and where you're not walking with Him. Unlike those good, God-loving people who have just quit, read the word and respond to what you've read. God longs for you to respond to Him.

WHERE DO YOU GO FROM HERE?

Here are some steps you can take to begin to grow more Biblically Formed:

---

54 Hebrews 4:12-13

READ

The Bible is no ordinary book; when you hold it in your hands, you're holding the very word of God. With the help of the Holy Spirit, the text is one of the greatest tools He has given you to fight sin.

There is no other book in the history of the world quite like it. The Bible is a collection of 66 books written over 1500 years by more than 40 different authors in 3 different languages, on multiple continents, and yet has a common theme: the glory of God and the redemption of mankind.

You could pick a book of the Bible and read through it or use a reading plan and systematically work through the entire thing in a year. It doesn't have to be long prayerful sessions. Take a few minutes and just read it. Pull out a notebook, write down what you read, and see what God does. "Your word I have treasured in my heart, that I may not sin against You."[55] A steady dose of the word of God on a regular basis begins to change who you are on the inside.

STUDY

Be diligent to present yourself approved to God as a workman who does not need to be ashamed, accurately

---

55 Psalm 119:11, NASB

handling the word of truth.[56]

Take the time to study the text, but be encouraged, the word of God was given that you might understand it. God never intended for the Bible to be a complete mystery, nor does He reserve true understanding for the spiritual elite.

Use a Bible dictionary, an atlas or a commentary. With the advance of technology, you have access to thousands of reference works to help you make sense of a text.

MEMORIZE

In the face of temptation, the incarnate God (Jesus Christ) quoted Deuteronomy from memory. How much more do you need the word of God readily available when faced with temptation?

Put a verse to memory: "How can a young man keep his way pure? By keeping *it* according to Your word."[57] The text brings to light the sin in your life. It gives you the strength to battle temptation, fight off insecurity and deal with the fears in your heart.

MEDITATE

Fill your mind with the word of God and let it begin to sink in. Let the text be a topic of discussion at the breakfast table

---

56 2 Timothy 2:15, NASB
57 Psalm 119:9, NASB

and when you're getting coffee at work. Let it shape the things you talk about at the gym and think about at night.

That's what Moses intended when he wrote, "You shall teach them diligently to your sons and shall talk of them when you sit in your house and when you walk by the way and when you lie down and when you rise up. You shall bind them as a sign on your hand and they shall be as frontals on your forehead. You shall write them on the doorposts of your house and on your gates."[58]

DISCUSS

Get together with others and discuss the word of God. "Iron sharpens iron, So one man sharpens another."[59] You can learn from those God has put in your life, enriched by their contribution and challenged by their perspective. Everyone has a story and these stories shape the way people see things, so take the time to gather around the word with people of various backgrounds. It can add tremendous color to a conversation and their response to the text may just challenge, and possibly change, your way of thinking for His glory.

---

58 Deuteronomy 6:7-9, NASB
59 Proverbs 27:17, NASB

CULTURALLY ENGAGED

MORALLY DISCERNING

INTENTIONAL BLESSING

SACRIFICIALLY GENEROUS

HUMBLY SUBMITTED

BIBLICALLY FORMED

RELATIONALLY HEALTHY

INCLUSIVE COMMUNITY

CHAPTER 7

SACRIFICIALLY GENEROUS

I LOVED MONDAY nights as a kid. In my home, it meant meatloaf and football. My dad would rummage through the kitchen and make meatloaf out of whatever he could find: bell peppers, onions, corn flakes, a few eggs. We would sit in front of the TV with a large bottle of ketchup and get after it, and those were the days.

I was pretty young, but I understood tickets to football games were not cheap, and hotel rooms and plane flights must have cost a fortune, and yet, every Monday night I saw Banner Man in the stands. Whatever he did for a living, I wanted that job. I was convinced he spent his Mondays traveling across the country just to hold up his John 3:16 banner. What a life. Game after game, rain, snow, or shine, he was faithfully there, reminding everyone his name was John, and he got stuck in the end zone again: row 3, seat 16.

Years later, I realized these faithful fans were trying to point people to Christ using one of the most over-quoted and underappreciated verses in the entire Bible.

> For God so loved the world, that he gave his only Son, that whoever believes in him should not perish but have eternal life.[60]

"For God so loved the world, that he gave." Jesus paid a price that you could never pay, and He provided redemption for you that you could never attain, and secured eternity for you that you could never earn. His riches were poured out for you and resulted in your glory. God gave, and because He gave, you should give.

Sadly, instead of building the Kingdom of God with your time, talent and treasures, you have become more consumed with building your own little castles. Do you think your own is your own?

The cattle on a thousand hills are His,[61] the earth and

---

60 John 3:16
61 Psalm 50:10

everything in it is His, all you have is His. Do you really think God, who set the world in motion and put the Earth on its axis, has given you the money you have so you can keep it for you? So you can buy a bigger boat, a better house, so you can look cool when you pull into Starbucks? Do you really think your time and talents are yours to use how you want? He is Lord of all, and He has entrusted it to you – all of it. You must recognize that none of it is yours to begin with or yours to control; it's yours to invest.

Everything you have is given so that you would give it away.

• • •

BUILD BIGGER BARNS, he thought.

And he told them a parable, saying, "The land of a rich man produced plentifully, and he thought to himself, 'What shall I do, for I have nowhere to store my crops?' And he said, 'I will do this: I will tear down my barns and build larger ones, and there I will store all my grain and my goods. And I will say to my soul, "Soul, you have ample goods laid up for many years; relax, eat, drink, be merry."' But God said to him, 'Fool! This night your soul is required of you, and the things you have prepared, whose will they be?'"[62]

How selfish and arrogant of this man to think his life was about him. There's nothing inherently wrong with being wealthy, and God never condemns the rich but challenges them: do not be conceited in wealth but give to the poor instead. God had provided, not for his comfort or ease or peace of mind, but so that he would be a blessing to others.

Jesus lived with the end in mind. He was a servant and very purposeful with His life, focusing on all that the Father had for Him to do. The Gospel of Mark uses "immediately" 36 times, giving the impression that Jesus didn't waste any time or meander aimlessly. He moved methodically through life, having purposeful

---

[62] Luke 12:16-20

encounters and intentional conversation. He was always evaluating, investing, and pouring out His time, talent and treasures for the betterment of others.

Jesus says, "But it shall not be so among you. But whoever would be great among you must be your servant, and whoever would be first among you must be slave of all. For even the Son of Man came not to be served but to serve, and to give his life as a ransom for many."[63] His calendar reflected His desire to give His life away and to give of His time. The more popular He became, the more difficult it was to find solitude.

> Jesus withdrew with his disciples to the sea, and a great crowd followed, from Galilee and Judea and Jerusalem and Idumea and from beyond the Jordan and from around Tyre and Sidon. When the great crowd heard all that he was doing, they came to him. And he told his disciples to have a boat ready for him because of the crowd, lest they crush him, for he had healed many, so that all who had diseases pressed around him to touch him.[64]

Unselfishly and without regret, Jesus continued to heal the people, teach the crowds, and invest what time had been entrusted to Him into others.

---

63 Mark 10:43-45
64 Mark 3:7-10

In the Gospel of Luke, messengers were sent to confirm Jesus was indeed the savior of the world.

And he answered them, "Go and tell John what you have seen and heard: the blind receive their sight, the lame walk, lepers are cleansed, and the deaf hear, the dead are raised up, the poor have good news preached to them. And blessed is the one who is not offended by me."[65]

Jesus moved from town to town and village to village performing miracles and teaching with profound authority, giving of His talent.

What about His treasures? Nearly broke and homeless, Jesus didn't have much to give from a worldly standard: no land or home to pass on, no inheritance to offer.

True generosity is not based upon the amount given but on the sacrificial nature of the gift.

"Truly, I say to you, this poor widow has put in more than all those who are contributing to the offering box. For they all contributed out of their abundance, but she out of her poverty has put in everything she had, all she had to live on."[66]

65 Luke 7:22-23
66 Mark 12:43-44

If the things you treasure are the things of this world, then that is where your heart will be. If the things you treasure are the things of God, then that is where your heart will be. Jesus says, "Do not lay up for yourselves treasures on earth, where moth and rust destroy and where thieves break in and steal, but lay up for yourselves treasures in heaven, where neither moth nor rust destroys and where thieves do not break in and steal. For where your treasure is, there your heart will be also."[67]

God gave, and what He gave was of the highest value: He offered Himself, providing salvation for all mankind for eternity to those who would believe by faith. He gave so you would be a blessing to others. He invested in you, entrusted things to you, and how should you respond?

• • •

---

67 Matthew 6:19-20

WHAT'S MINE is yours. Take it.

Giving is not easy, and in many lives selfishness and materialism have replaced generosity. Why is there so much joy and contentment in the slums of Nairobi, Kenya, or in the streets of Costa Rica, or among the impoverished of Thailand? Simplicity. Life is simple, and the things of concern are food, water and shelter. In our culture, most people just want more, and regardless of how much they have, they are still trying to accumulate more. More money, more time, more influence. There's a constant thirst and hunger for more, and more never makes anyone happy, but life is always about the next bigger and better thing: the next two hundred dollar pair of jeans, the next car lease, the next nip and tuck.

Are you trying to buy your way to happiness? If so, you have probably squandered a significant opportunity to express sacrificial generosity to those around you.

He gives to you so that you would give it away. Do you believe that? Your stuff, your opportunities, your gifts, and your money are for others. Whatever God has given to you, give it away. Test God and see if He won't indeed open up the storehouses of heaven,[68] but that doesn't mean you give so God will bless you. Tell that to Job. You give so God will give you more, so you can give more.

_____
68 Malachi 3:10

"…give, and it will be given to you. Good measure, pressed down, shaken together, running over, will be put into your lap. For with the measure you use it will be measured back to you."[69]

What has God given to you? Better said, what has God entrusted to you?

What about your time? Who gets your best and what gets your scraps? You say you value God above everything else, but your time goes to everything else but God. You make time for a six-pack and huge arms, Botox and the health spa, but you're spiritually bankrupt on the inside. What would it look like to say no, to thin your life of superfluous activity? Is your calendar filled with activities out of obligation? Generosity with your time is very difficult when you don't have a lot of it, so slow your life down by having boundaries, and live with a sense of a higher calling.

Why are you here? Did God give you breath to build castles, or to point people toward Jesus and make disciples? You're to bring glory and honor to God, and He has made you for that purpose. Recognize that your talents are for others, and the best of who you are should be given to the things of God. What are you good at, and how can you use it to benefit others? Maybe it's baking birthday cakes, writing resumes or delivering donuts to the school office.

---

69 Luke 6:38

I'm really good at lifting things, but I purposely avoided buying a truck in college because I didn't want to help my buddies move every weekend. You know what I wish now? I wish I had a truck so I can help my buddies move. Why? Because I want to have a heart that's Humbly Submitted to God, to read what God says about caring for the people around me, and to be Sacrificially Generous with everything He has entrusted to me.

If you're faithful in the little things, God will entrust true riches to you to be used for His glory. Do you say no and merely take care of yourself? Are you still trying to impress people by how you dress or what you drive? There's no joy in your life if you're living beyond your means. Why? Joy comes from giving, not receiving, and it's very difficult to be generous when you're in debt. Most people live their lives completely leveraged, spend more than they make, and wonder why they're so stressed. The treasures you pursue should not be of this world, "but seek first the kingdom of God and his righteousness, and all these things will be added to you."[70]

Where do you find that God designed you to accumulate, compare or compete? There is no freedom in busyness, no freedom in hoarding your gifts and abilities, and certainly no freedom when you're a lenders' slave.

God will give you what you need, feed you with the food

---

[70] Matthew 6:33

that is your portion, and the rest – just give it away.

WHERE DO YOU GO FROM HERE?

Here are some steps you can take to begin to grow more Sacrificially Generous:

BIG ROCKS

I have three things I try to do every day, and I call them my big rocks: read the word, spend time with family and work out, and these hit my calendar first. What does your calendar look like? What do you value and where do you spend your time? Make sure you're investing time into the things that truly matter.

TAKE INVENTORY

What stuff could you give away or let someone borrow? What opportunities do you have? What talents? Who could benefit from what you've been gifted?

10 – 10 – 80

10%. Take the next six months and give away 10 percent of everything you earn. Be creative. Find organizations you trust, churches you believe in, and friends in need. Pray about where God wants His money, and then enjoy the process of giving it away.

10%. Take the next six months and pay yourself 10 percent of what you earn. Set it aside in a savings account and watch it grow. Set a goal and when you reach it, reward yourself.

80%. Take the next six months and learn to live off of what is left. Set a budget and live simply. When you live within your means, you'll feel the freedom to give generously.

CHAPTER 8

INTENTIONAL BLESSING

JESUS ENTERED into the pigsty of humanity, died between two thieves, and gave the ultimate gift to you: "Greater love has no one than this, that someone lay down his life for his friends."[71]

When Jesus had received the sour wine, he said, "It is finished," and he bowed his head and gave up his spirit.[72]

All He did, He did on purpose for you, on your behalf – riches poured out for you, resulting in your glory. Take your time, talents and treasures and invest them into the people around you *on purpose.* Why? Because that's what Jesus did.

---

71 John 15:13
72 John 19:30

What is the greatest commandment?

And he said to him, "You shall love the Lord your God with all your heart and with all your soul and with all your mind. This is the great and first commandment. And a second is like it: You shall love your neighbor as yourself."[73]

So who are your neighbors?

"A man was going down from Jerusalem to Jericho, and he fell among robbers, who stripped him and beat him and departed, leaving him half dead. Now by chance a priest was going down that road, and when he saw him he passed by on the other side. So likewise a Levite, when he came to the place and saw him, passed by on the other side. But a Samaritan, as he journeyed, came to where he was, and when he saw him, he had compassion. He went to him and bound up his wounds, pouring on oil and wine. Then he set him on his own animal and brought him to an inn and took care of him."[74]

Do you get it? The way you show love for God and your neighbor is by being an Intentional Blessing. The Levite and the Priest turn down an opportunity to show love for God as if there are people you should and shouldn't love. They just pass by thinking,

73 Matthew 22:37-39
74 Luke 10:30-34

that's going to be expensive; that's going to be a mess. The Samaritan comes along and bandages his wounds, gives him medicine, carries him by horse to a nearby city, puts him up until he's well, and pays for all his expenses. The Levite, the Priest or the Samaritan: which one proved to be a neighbor?

In a similar fashion, as Peter and John approached the Temple, they walked by a disabled man sitting in the road. Disabled from birth, the man was excluded from worshipping with his community, and his circumstance would have put his family in significant poverty. As Peter and John passed by, he asked them for some change.

But Peter said, "I have no silver and gold, but what I do have I give to you. In the name of Jesus Christ of Nazareth, rise up and walk!"[75]

Immediately upon restoration, he enters the temple for the first time in his life and worships God.

"For the Son of Man came to seek and to save the lost."[76] The example of Christ was to intentionally pursue those who were in need.

• • •

75 Acts 3:6
76 Luke 19:10

FOR DAYS, I had tried to avoid eye contact with him. He sat on the street corner, unkept and disheveled, with a cardboard sign that read: Anything will help. I would pass him on my way to work, not convinced that just *anything* would really *help*. If I gave him some money what would he use it for? Would he buy food, clothing, a blanket or a fifth of vodka? Call me calloused, but my skepticism was high.

He was there with that sign, day after day. I wondered, *where did he come from? Where did he sleep? Did he have any family? What did he really need?* But then the light would turn green, and I would awkwardly move on. I hate that feeling. I knew I didn't have the means to get him off of the streets or get back on his feet. So what could I really do? I could scrounge for some change or toss him my sack lunch, but these tokens wouldn't truly change his life. Maybe it's not about changing his life. Maybe it's about brightening his day, showing kindness and showing the love of Christ.

One day, instead of awkwardly moving on, I pulled over and invited him to lunch. Over a sloppy burger and some fries, I heard his story. He had lost his job, was evicted from his apartment, and had turned to drugs and alcohol. The cycle of misfortune and bad decisions continued, and he ended up on a street corner. He had hoped that his life would be different. He had grand dreams of starting a business and carving out a good living for himself. Instead he was stuck, just holding that sign.

I seriously doubt that our interaction over a burger changed his life, but I know that it brightened his day. I didn't have much, but what I had, I gave freely.

Drop the waitress a nice tip, or take warm chocolate chip cookies four houses down to the neighbor you've never met. Maybe it's the guy next door whose weeds are trees, and you chop down his forest. Pick up someone else's tab and sneak out the back door. Borrow a truck and help a friend move. Open up your home. Support someone on a mission trip, or partner financially with an organization. Leave a bag of groceries at your neighbor's front door or donuts for you kids' teachers, and just drive away. Just be a blessing.

Being a blessing is completely counter-cultural, for it comes at a cost. But if it costs you nothing, is it really love?

Intentional Blessing is an authenticator of true faith. If you have a heart Humbly Submitted to God and a mind shaped by His word, and you recognize your stuff is His, spiritual growth will begin to spill out into the area of compassion, and you will be a blessing to others on purpose. Now you're living on the edge, in the outer ring.

Become aware of what God is already doing around you, discern the needs you see, and pray for direction. Once you begin to see the opportunities God has purposely put before you, take the initiative to be a blessing in someone else's life. Remember, people in your life have issues, hurts and backstories, and though you may only see them for a moment, recognize the potential impact you may have on their day. Smile, be polite, and show them Christ.

Fulfillment comes from serving, and once you get your eyes off of yourself and leverage what God has given you for the betterment of others, you will find contentment and happiness. Don't become overwhelmed or paralyzed by the needs of the many that you do nothing. Not every need you see demands a personal response, but recognize God wants something from you. He gave, and now that you've got it, what are you going to do with it?

WHERE DO YOU GO FROM HERE?

Here are some steps you can take to begin to grow more in the way of Intentional Blessing:

LOOK AROUND

What would it look like for you to live out Sacrificially Generous on purpose right where God has put you? Is there someone you can help? Maybe it's a neighbor, friend, colleague or classmate. Get creative. Maybe it's a few dollars, a sandwich or a bag of groceries.

WHAT'S IN YOUR TOOLBOX?

Do you have a unique skillset that could benefit someone? Maybe you can provide counsel or advice, change oil in a car or fix a squeaky door.

START SMALL

Have you considered raking your neighbor's leaves or pulling in their trash cans? It doesn't have to be profound. It just needs to be something. Try giving out really good Halloween candy or sponsoring a child overseas. Bring donuts to your child's teacher or say, "Thank you," to a member of the armed forces.

PAY IT FORWARD

Every time Kathryn went to Starbucks, she bought a cup of coffee for the person in line behind her, and while it wasn't much, it brightened someone's day. Be faithful in the little things, recognizing what you can't do for everyone, you can do for one.

CHAPTER 9

MORALLY DISCERNING

I WAS IN COLLEGE in the early '90s and it was a time of Pearl Jam and Nirvana and flannel shirts. Rage Against the Machine had just dropped their self-titled album, and they slew me instantly with their provocative sound and lyrics.

At the time, I was living in Sigma Chi's fraternity house, far from the Lord and focused on things that stimulated all sorts of decoration and other nonsense. In particular, our classic WWII-themed party where we covered the floor with sand and every inch of wall with greenery to resemble a forest in Normandy, if one even existed. However, we were broke and couldn't afford sand or greenery, so we went shrubbing. That's what we called it. We spent months shrubbing around town in pickups, stealing as many trees, vines and shrubs as possible from front yards.

Then I came to faith in Christ.

It was March 1993, right before Sigma Chi's biggest party week of the year. The party itinerary came out and the headliner band read: Knucklehead, a Rage-inspired funk metal band. And I wanted to go. I had moved out of the fraternity, and my new roommates, who were solid followers of Christ, tried to talk me out of it. I had begun to grow spiritually and was really excited to help my friends come to faith in Christ, and I was torn.

As soon as I showed up, drinks were offered, and I said no at first, but they kept coming. I wanted a way to connect with my friends and maybe earn some credibility, so I began to reason with myself. *I'm of age. I can keep it under control. I don't want to be that guy who can't relate or be in their world. I can have a beer or two.* One led to two, two led me to a shot, and then to another, which eventually led me to passing out drunk. I was a young Christian, and all alone, I walked into temptation and I got crushed. It was an area I had struggled with considerably in my not-so-distant past, and not strong enough to fight it or wise enough to run, I was completely wrecked and lost all credibility. What an embarrassment I was. Every conversation put into question by my sin, and my voice was muted. No one heard me now. I had claimed Christ and then lived like that, and that's not what Jesus is about. So why would my friends become Christians? Christians are drunks.

When was the last time you really blew it spiritually? I'm willing to bet you had the same thought process I did, and it happens more times than you care to admit. Why? You lack moral discernment. You put yourself in bad situations, usually all alone, with disregard to godly counsel, and think you can handle it. It's not surprising when you surround yourself with compromise that you soon become compromised yourself.

Do not be deceived: "Bad company ruins good morals."[77]

Moral discernment is choice, and choice is a direct outcome of what's happening inside. You can't blame culture or your friends or unfortunate circumstance for your bad choices. The problem is you. James put it this way, "But each person is tempted when he is lured and enticed by his own desire."[78] What's happening in your heart? Does His desire supersede yours? His will for your life trump yours? Don't deceive yourself into thinking you're living for you. You're living for Christ, and who you are and what you do reflect Him, and your choices and behaviors affirm your faith or erode your credibility. He created only one *you* for a reason and strategically placed you right where you are, and then put people in your life He wants you to influence for His glory.

• • •

---

77 1 Corinthians 15:33
78 James 1:14

"THEY'RE OUT OF WINE," His mother said to Him on the third day of the feast.[79]

John tells us that Jesus, His mother and His disciples were invited to attend a wedding in the city of Cana. Weddings in that day were excessive celebrations and Middle Eastern hospitality was such that to run out of wine was a significant disgrace. Jesus quickly had the servants gather six stone pots and fill them to the brim with water, each holding 20 to 30 gallons, and then He turned the water into wine. Not just wine, but really good wine, and so much so, that the master of the feast asked the bride and groom why they saved the good stuff for last.

In Matthew, Jesus says:

For John came neither eating nor drinking, and they say, "He has a demon." The Son of Man came eating and drinking, and they say, "Look at him! A glutton and a drunkard, a friend of tax collectors and sinners."[80]

Did Jesus have a glass of wine? The text doesn't tell you, although you would assume He did. Drinking wine didn't have the same social stigma in the first century that it does today, but don't miss my point. I'm not suggesting Jesus was drunk, but I'm saying He brought 120 gallons of really good wine to a party. I'm

79 See John 2:3
80 Matthew 11:18-19

suggesting He entered into culture.

As a young Christian, I went to church and met people whose first names were either Brother or Sister, and they said things like "Be in the world but not of the world," and "God works all things for the good,"[81] and "Just pray about it," and they hung out in Christian bookstores and coffee shops. They didn't live in the world I lived in. They definitely didn't speak my language and had no idea how to reach me or my friends. Everyone kept smiling, no one ever listened to secular music or watched R-rated movies, and I'm pretty sure these people here were overly concerned about what I wore. This was not the Jesus I knew.

The Jesus I read about hung out in seedy places with shady people, and these were His friends. He was provocative and unpredictable, and He drove religious people crazy, and I could imagine the stories He must have told at the dinner table and the laughter that filled the room.

After this he went out and saw a tax collector named Levi, sitting at the tax booth. And he said to him, "Follow me." And leaving everything, he rose and followed him. And Levi made him a great feast in his house, and there was a large company of tax collectors and others reclining at table with them. And the Pharisees and their scribes grumbled at

81 See Romans 8:28

97

his disciples, saying, "Why do you eat and drink with tax collectors and sinners?" And Jesus answered them, "Those who are well have no need of a physician, but those who are sick. I have not come to call the righteous but sinners to repentance."[82]

In Matthew, Jesus takes His disciples on a three-day hike north from the Sea of Galilee to the city of Caesarea Philippi, a hub for idolatry, worshipping both Caesar as well as Pan, a supposed god of the underworld believed to be half-goat and half-man. The people would practice various types of immorality, some of which included sexual intercourse with a goat, to entice Pan from the abyss and arouse him to bring fertility to the land.

So why would Jesus take His disciples to first-century Las Vegas?

Now when Jesus came into the district of Caesarea Philippi, he asked his disciples, "Who do people say that the Son of Man is?" And they said, "Some say John the Baptist, others say Elijah, and others Jeremiah or one of the prophets."

He said to them, "But who do you say that I am?" Simon Peter replied, "You are the Christ, the Son of the living God."

---

82 Luke 5:27-32

And Jesus answered him, "Blessed are you, Simon Bar-Jonah! For flesh and blood has not revealed this to you, but my Father who is in heaven. And I tell you, you are Peter, and on this rock I will build my church, and the gates of hell shall not prevail against it. I will give you the keys of the kingdom of heaven, and whatever you bind on earth shall be bound in heaven, and whatever you loose on earth shall be loosed in heaven."[83]

Jesus took His disciples into this city to make the point that He is the cornerstone of the church, and built upon Him, the darkest places on earth will not overcome it, not even the dirty, middle-of-nowhere city of Caesarea Philippi.

He took them into dark places to make them uncomfortable, forcing them to use moral discernment, and He took them because they represented Him.

Again Jesus spoke to them, saying, "I am the light of the world. Whoever follows me will not walk in darkness, but will have the light of life."[84]

You're the light of the world and light shines in darkness, but if light never goes into darkness, how can it be light? As a follower of Christ, you're called to be godly among the ungodly.

83 Matthew 16:13-19
84 John 8:12

Throughout the Gospels, Jesus came to the defense of the broken, restored the sick, gave grace to the immoral, valued the Samaritan, cleared the temple so the Gentiles could worship, and tirelessly opposed looking good on the outside while being dirty on the inside. He lived in perfect obedience to the Father in an imperfect world, and He lived His life in fluidity, never anchored in legalism nor lulled to license. Jesus interacted with less than perfect people, and He entered into culture, each time without compromise, and He's calling you to go and exercise similar moral discernment.

• • •

WHAT IS OFF-LIMITS and what are you allowed to do? Moral discernment can't be rule-setting in a static life because your life is rarely predictable. Is it right for you to go or not? Have a drink or not? Stay the night or not? It depends. Once you say that, the rules are broken, and let's be honest, you're terrible at thinking on your feet.

Moral discernment is not a rule-driven thing; it's a submission-to-God thing.

Check Your Heart – Ask the why. What's your motivation? What's the desired outcome?

Check the Scriptures – Does the Bible have anything to say about your decision? If so, do what it says. You must be obedient to the text where the scriptures speak, but if the text is silent or vague, then you're going to have to flex your Morally Discerning muscle.

Once your heart is submitted to God, moral discernment flows through the scriptures, and as you become skilled in using the text, it's learned over time, with constant practice to distinguish good from evil. Life will ebb and flow, and you will constantly have to adjust, so it might be totally fine to do one thing one day and not the next. Still not sure?

Get Wise Counsel – The bigger the issue, or the greyer, the more you need additional wisdom. If it's a simple decision, make the call. However, if it has big implications, seek out advice from a trusted source.

Be Mindful of the Weaker Brother – Just because you can, doesn't mean you should. A sign of spiritual maturity is to look out for the weaker brother. Paul uses the phrase "weaker brother" repeatedly in 1 Corinthians to refer to someone who is less spiritually mature, and would not understand or agree with your behavior. If your actions would cause someone else to potentially stumble, maybe you shouldn't flex your freedom.

The issue you're wrestling with is permission, and it can't be legalism, meaning you can't live by preset rules and guidelines, nor can it be license, meaning freedom to express yourself without thought of the text or considering your weaker brother. Moral discernment is like having a game plan and making half-time adjustments. You need to learn to make decisions when life happens, and you need to think biblically.

> For though by this time you ought to be teachers, you
> need someone to teach you again the basic principles of the
> oracles of God. You need milk, not solid food, for everyone
> who lives on milk is unskilled in the word of righteousness,
> since he is a child. But solid food is for the mature, for

those who have their powers of discernment trained by constant practice to distinguish good from evil.[85]

There must come a time when you are weaned from milk and press on to solid food. A believer matures when they turn to the word of God for guidance, and then the word of God is no longer baby food, but solid, sustaining, spiritual nourishment.

• • •

---

85 Hebrews 5:12-14

YOU GET UP in the morning and do life. Sometimes you do it well, sometimes not, and for the most part, you fight your way through the day rushing from here to there with little thought given to what God wants for you. You throw down some beers with the boys, gossip at the water cooler or look at pornography, or you spend the weekend with your girlfriend or boyfriend at the coast, and think, *what does it matter?*

That's indifference.

After I had fallen at Sigma Chi's party, literally passed out drunk, I stood in front of 50 sorority girls and apologized because I realized what I do matters. Christ was dishonored and I felt so convicted, and I had underestimated how my decisions wrecked my reputation.

What you do, how you live, and the decisions you make matter. God wants you to be a part of something, and you need to see that. He's starting in your heart, and once your heart is His and your mind is filtered through His word, you will begin to see life differently. God has a calling on your life to make an impact, and when you're growing in the area of moral discernment, you have influence on those around you. Your life has volume. God wants to use you to influence others, so live in a manner that gives you credibility to say something and be heard.

You can't influence culture if you're removed from it, and you can't go into these dark places if your heart and mind are not right, and my point is, you might need to go. That might be exactly where God wants you, but only you can make that call.

WHERE DO YOU GO FROM HERE?

Here are some steps you can take to begin to grow more Morally Discerning:

CONSTANT PRACTICE

Think of a few scenarios in your life and use the following progression of decision-making detailed in this chapter to see how it affects your actions.

Check Your Heart
Check the Scriptures
Get Wise Counsel
Be Mindful of the Weaker Brother

LEGALISM VERSUS LICENSE

Think about areas in your life where the decisions you make are either pre-determined or expressions of freedom, or areas where you do what you want without thought of the text or your weaker brother.

DOES YOUR LIFE SHINE?

Do you find yourself gravitating to the safe, comfortable places in life? Remember, there's nothing safe or comfortable about incarnation. It was incarnation that changed the world. Jesus went into unsafe, unpredictable places, and He might be calling you to do the same.

Where have you chosen isolation over incarnation?

WHAT YOU DO MATTERS

God is at work, even now, exposing indifference in your life. Do you see the opportunities God has given you to influence those around you toward Christ?

CHAPTER 10

CULTURALLY ENGAGED

I TRAVELED TO BANGKOK, Thailand on a six-week mission trip with my friend Mike Slayden in the summer of '97. It was there I told him I was seriously thinking about planting a church someday, and I asked if he would pray about coming with me.

When I first met Mike, he was a student at the University of North Texas, a member of the local Sigma Nu fraternity, and had recently come to faith in Christ. We connected at Denton Bible Church where I was serving at the time, and we became fast friends and did what we could to encourage others to grow spiritually. While technically I was discipling Mike, I think he was actually discipling me.

Five years after our Thailand trip, I started The Well Community Church in Fresno, California, and I called Mike. Moving away from home was not his first choice, but feeling called by God to go, he and his wife packed up their two girls, left Texas and headed west.

Mike and I share similar backgrounds, and a passion for coffee and long bike rides. We would ride for hours and talk about life, the church, our marriages and our kids. That is, until we rode uphill. Mike was super fit and I was a Clydesdale; when we climbed, he talked while I just tried not to pass out. Most of the good decisions we made were done wearing spandex.

During his tenure at The Well, Mike has held many titles: Teaching Pastor, Campus Pastor, Equipping Director, Small Groups Director and Residency Director. He was a great leader and an even better friend, but he began to feel discontent. He enjoyed what he did but something was missing. Never truly satisfied, and struggling to find his sweet spot, it began to strain our friendship, until one day he called and said, "I finally know what God wants me to do."

I was curious to hear him pitch his next new position at The Well. He came over, and we sat on my back porch with the sun in our face. "I want to resign," he said.

"What?" I was shocked.

For the next few hours, he talked about starting a non-profit ministry that would help impoverished children in our community. He wanted to motivate kids toward a healthy lifestyle and reward them with bicycles for their progress in academics, character and service. Mike and bicycles made sense. Mike and the underserved areas of our city didn't. Quit a good job and help the impoverished? Who does that? Especially not a kid who grew up in North Dallas where what matters most is the crystal in your watch and the shine in your shoes.

• • •

CRAZY LARRY WAS his name. In Israel, in the ruins of Susita, overlooking the eastern shores of the Sea of Galilee, I listened to my friend PJ Lewis share the story of a demon-possessed man. Throughout his teaching, he called the outcast Crazy Larry. Rejected by family and friends, Crazy Larry lived in the caves of Susita and was tormented by a legion of demons. Day and night he cried out from the tombs and cut himself, and if anyone tried to subdue him, he would break free from his chains and give them an old-fashioned beat down.

Modern Susita reveals only burnt-out barracks and abandoned Syrian bunkers taken by the Israelis in the Six Days War. However, recent excavations have uncovered beautiful mosaic floors, a theatre, an ancient water system, and the city dump where remnants of pig bones were found. This discovery suggests the city was not a Jewish city but rather a city of the pagan. In fact, it was a city in the Decapolis, an area of ten prominent Greek cities in the time of Christ associated with pagan worship and the sacrificing of pigs. If you were a God-fearing Jew, you wouldn't come to the Decapolis.

But Jesus did come.

The demons, recognizing Jesus was the Son of God, pleaded for mercy and asked that they be sent into the pigs feeding on the hillside instead of being sent into the abyss. Jesus granted their request, and the demons entered the pigs and plunged them down the hillside to their death.

When the people of the city heard they had lost their income, as well as potential offerings to their deities, they came to confront Jesus. To their amazement, having a meal on the shore with Jesus was Crazy Larry, clothed and in his right mind. Not quite sure what to do with Jesus, they asked Him to leave, and Crazy Larry wanted to go with Him. Ready for a fresh start, he wanted to leave the pain and regret of Susita behind, but Jesus said no.

And he did not permit him but said to him, "Go home to your friends and tell them how much the Lord has done for you, and how he has had mercy on you." And he went away and began to proclaim in the Decapolis how much Jesus had done for him, and everyone marveled.[86]

After some time, Jesus returned to the Decapolis and while there, a great crowd assembled.

In those days, when again a great crowd had gathered, and they had nothing to eat, he called his disciples to him and said to them, "I have compassion on the crowd, because they have been with me now three days and have nothing

---

86 Mark 5:19-20

to eat. And if I send them away hungry to their homes, they will faint on the way. And some of them have come from far away."[87]

Why did these people come to see Jesus, and how did they hear about Him? Could it have been Crazy Larry?

• • •

---

87 Mark 8:1-3

WHO AM I?

I played football at Fresno State, so now I serve as the team chaplain. My mom left, and then my stepmom left, and that's why I'm so passionate about marriage, and why I'm committed to raising two daughters who don't have a father wound. My brother Dan was a drug addict. First it was pot, then alcohol, and when he moved to cocaine, the torment got worse. I didn't ask for it and I didn't want it, but God allowed me to go through it.

God made me who I am. Who I am in Christ matters because He has something for me to do.

Why Crazy Larry? Why Abraham or Noah? Why would David, the youngest son of Jesse and a runt shepherd boy, be anointed king? It's what God wanted. Why Peter an apostle to the Jews, and Paul an apostle to the Gentiles? Why Moses to lead the people out of Egypt and into the desert for 40 years? It's what God wanted, though it made no sense to others. God prepared them to do exactly what He wanted them to do.

For we are his workmanship, created in Christ Jesus for good works, which God prepared beforehand, that we should walk in them.[88]

---

88 Ephesians 2:10

That *you* would walk in them. The way *you* live matters, and God has created *you* for a profound purpose. He is in control of all things and He doesn't waste any motion. Everything in your life is allowed to happen to prepare you for something. What is that something? It's the "good works" that He prepared beforehand so *you* would walk in them.

What have you been through? How can God use it for His own glory? God never wastes an opportunity, and you may be surprised by what He has for you. He may open doors that don't seem to make sense.

Experiences – See Christ in a fresh way through your brokenness. Do you truly understand what others are going through? Can you empathize with their pain and share in their victories? For example, my brother Dan came to faith in Christ, and his journey of sobriety led him into a leadership position at Celebrate Recovery, a local ministry in town that helps people get and stay sober.

Think about your experiences differently. Do they give you access to a group of people others can't reach?

Passions – What do you love? What excites you? "Delight yourself in the Lord, and he will give you the desires of your heart." This doesn't mean He will deliver everything to you like a genie in a bottle. This means your desires are from Him, and your relationship with Christ will bring passions to you. He isn't going to call you into a ministry you hate. For example, if you don't like kids, stay out of the nursery.

Spiritual Gifts – Some serve, some lead, some teach, and others give hugs. God has gifted you. Do you know what your gifts are? Know them and develop them, but you can't develop what you're not aware of: "Take pains with these things; be absorbed in them, so that your progress will be evident to all."[89]

Personality – You are "fearfully and wonderfully made."[90] Are you a people-person? Find an area where you can work with others. Do you like to crunch numbers? Find an administrative position where you can help an extrovert organize his or her life.

Experiences. Write them down. Passions. Write them down. Spiritual gifts and personality traits, write them down. Slow down and take the time to think it through, and do it now. If you put it all on a page, you might be able to clearly connect the dots and think, *here it is. This makes perfect sense.* If it's not clear, it might at least point you in a certain direction.

In Mike's life, moral discernment had moved beyond indifference. He knew that his life mattered, and God had works He

---

89 1 Timothy 4:15, NASB
90 Psalm 139:14

wanted Mike to be a part of. Mike's heart was Humbly Submitted and his mind Biblically Formed, and he knew God had a plan for his life. God had strategically placed passions in his heart, and as Mike prayed about what God had for him, the dots started to point somewhere. Mike loved fitness, and as his passion came out, he thought, *maybe I'll go get involved with that.* His tenure as a pastor, his education, his love of bike riding, even his North Dallas upbringing prepared him for this: to launch a non-profit called Off The Front.[91]

At some point in your life, God will lay something on your heart, and He will not leave it alone. For Mike, it was childhood obesity, and it had subtly shifted from *someone should do something about that* to *I should do something about that.* God was at work at his very core, and his spiritual growth was spilling out into the area of compassion, and he began to live more Culturally Engaged. It was awareness, then brokenness that moved him to action. He saw things differently, and he realized it was his personal responsibility to meet the needs of his city, and God had strategically positioned him to move. He had to step up. He had no choice. It was as if God would grant him no rest until he got personally involved.

What does Culturally Engaged look like for you?

There are many who won't engage culture, who are afraid, who are waiting for a voice from heaven to cry out and the skies to

---

91 offthefront.org

open up and reveal the vision of God. Sitting on the sidelines and doing nothing is not an option because He has things for you to do. You learn more about yourself and who God made you to be through failure. Any good coach would tell you: if you're going to make a mistake, make it at full speed. The best lessons are learned through failure, and it's trial and error, so get moving and do something. If God has you where He wants you to be, you will feel fulfilled and be fruitful. If not, He will show you where He wants you to go. Again, become aware of what God is doing in your life. There are many things you can do but only a few things you must do.

WHERE DO YOU GO FROM HERE?

Here are some steps you can take to begin to grow more Culturally Engaged:

WHO ARE YOU?

Find out who God made you to be, and be good at being you. What have you suffered through? God may have orchestrated affliction in your life so you can reach others in similar places. What gets you fired up? Has God placed anything on your heart that you must be a part of?

START SOMEWHERE

I've found it's easier to determine what God wants you to do when you're actually out there doing something. Find a place to serve, get involved, donate time or contribute in some way. You will not be able to help everyone, but you can do something for someone. You could start with your church, and most churches have tons of service opportunities that may fit your specific area of passion, as well as contact with other ministries and organizations in your community.

Then pray about it. Ask God to show you what He has prepared for you.

TAKE AN OFF-RAMP

Longevity and joy in ministry are intimately connected to your personal passions, and as they change, change with them. Become aware of what God is doing and follow Him there. All you need is a humble heart, a mind filtered through His word, and a willingness to say yes to God when He lays something on your heart that wrecks you. God may re-wire you to do something different now and again, so be flexible and go with it.

INVITE OTHERS IN

It's not just about what you do but the people you do it with. Share what you're doing with others, and as you're serving, invite them to be a part of it. When you share your passion and talk about stories of life change, your excitement can be contagious and others will want to get involved. Doing life with others makes being Culturally Engaged that much more fun.

CHAPTER 11

RELATIONALLY HEALTHY

YOU'RE PUNCH DRUNK with information about other people, and you long for your own followers, for ways to increase your friends and for people to like your stuff. Facebook. Twitter. Instagram. You're hyper-connected and constantly moving, just waiting to tell people what you're doing so that they can be impressed. This move toward virtual relationships has allowed life to be become filtered and censored, and more concerning, inauthentic. Very seldom do you see or hear something average or everyday. It's typically something fantastic and self-promoting. It's the constant deluge of selfies. *Here's how cool I am. And this is what I'm doing right now. Aren't you jealous? Don't you see how witty and brilliant I am in 140 characters?* Technology today has allowed more virtual connections than ever before, but are you really more connected? You're texting, pinning, tweeting, posting, liking, commenting and hash-tagging, and all the while, you're still unsatisfied and lonely. Why? Because there's no substitute for human interaction.

Engrossed in yourself, are you missing the opportunities for relational connection that God has for you? You're rushed and distracted, and the faster you go, the less you really see. The notion of slowing down seems both unproductive and utterly fruitless. However, friendships are about shared experience with reciprocation, and are cultivated over time. But who has an abundance of that?

You wake up when the alarm goes off so you can get to work, and you make phone calls while dropping your kids off at school. You hit the treadmill to work off lunch, then you're off to soccer this and dance that, and the dinner table is now the backseat of your car, all the while still making phone calls. Your front porch has been replaced by the backyard, and the backyard surrounded by privacy fences. You throw your kids to the digital babysitter so you can finish a few emails. You're mad they didn't get their homework done, but you were too busy shopping online or managing your fantasy football team to help. You go to bed and wake up at 5 a.m. the next morning to do the same thing all over again.

Jesus lived when there were no modern amenities or

creature comforts, when families shared a common courtyard, all cramped together in one place, every day.

All of life happened in one room: a 20 by 20 living space with no interior walls and no doors. They ate, fought, disciplined their children and enjoyed intimacy without the luxury of a locked door. They woke up when the sun rose, and the boys went to work with their fathers in the vineyards, farming figs, wheat and dates, and the daughters were with their mothers preparing lunch and dinner. No one read a book about manhood; they saw manhood every day. There would have been an open fire to bake bread and oil lamps to light the room when the sun went down – no running water or toilet, no door to slam or television to watch. Over a meal, multi-generations shared experience, grandpas and grandmas telling stories, and questions being asked about life before going to bed.

Do you feel sorry for them? I imagine they would feel sorry for you.

• • •

JESUS WAS PRESENT. He listened, empathized, entered in, and did life with those around Him. When the crowds pressed in to the point of crushing Him, and when the children gathered around Him, He spoke kindly and He taught. He saw interruptions as opportunities and awkward interactions as divine moments. For example, He asked the woman at the well for a drink, not because He was thirsty, but to enter in. He had a conversation with her because He is others-focused. Though busy, He was never rushed.

> And when he returned to Capernaum after some days, it was reported that he was at home. And many were gathered together, so that there was no more room, not even at the door. And he was preaching the word to them. And they came, bringing to him a paralytic carried by four men. And when they could not get near him because of the crowd, they removed the roof above him, and when they had made an opening, they let down the bed on which the paralytic lay.[92]

Jesus waited patiently, brushing the falling debris from his face, and He didn't yell or sigh in frustration as they dug their way through the roof. He didn't even get out of the way. His teaching was interrupted as these men lowered their friend down into the crowd, a feat that could have taken at least a half hour. Moved by

---

92 Mark 2:1-4

their intense expression of friendship, Jesus forgave and healed the man.

Jesus was surrounded by religious leaders who claimed to love God but had no love for their neighbor. However, these men demonstrated their love for God through loving their friend, and recognizing their great faith, He commends them.

Jesus was constantly looking for opportunities to invest in others. It was the normal, everyday things that made His relationships so rich: meals, fishing and hiking, throwing a good party, telling great stories, and laughing unreservedly and loudly with His friends. He never got His food to go or ate in His car, and was constantly reclining at a table, ordering appetizers, and simply taking His time. He saw meals as an unrushed way to get to know those around Him, and He saw people in need of real connection. It was never about taking care of Himself. Every moment of every day, He took initiative in the lives of others.

• • •

I WOKE UP TO freshly squeezed orange juice, was handed a brown bag lunch, and drove my girlfriend to school.

After my stepmom left, my dad took a job in Los Angeles for a season, and I was living with my girlfriend and her family while in high school. I experienced incredible culture shock. Her dad would sit and read the newspaper, and they would have dinner together at a table. Hers was a wonderful family with a kind of marriage I had never seen. It was what I had always imagined the American family to be, and I mourned the fact that I didn't have one. My mom had left when I was 9 years old and my brother was headed to rehab, my dad had several girlfriends, and after a brief stint with a stepmom, I was desperate for a good example of relational health.

I've listened to people order their morning coffee in between sentences with the person on their phone, too busy to smile or interact, and when interrupted hold up a finger as if to say shush, tersely repeating their order with a sigh of frustration before huffing away. And I've known people who were in relationships just to get their needs met: takers.

I've watched married couples spend an entire meal looking at their phones, inadvertently telling each other: this marriage is not nearly as important as furthering my online connection with everyone else. Your relationship with your spouse *is* your relationship with God. So when you date your spouse, you honor God.

Your relationship with God is intimately connected to your relationship with your family. Perhaps in order for you to get right with the Lord, you need to get right with your husband or wife or kids. You can have quiet times till Jesus comes, but until your family relationships are okay, God and you aren't okay. Who told you the goal of marriage was to be happy? If you love the Lord, but don't like your spouse, I don't really think you love the Lord. If you claim to be a follower of Christ your faith should be seen in the health of your relationships.

Everyone who reads this book has some sort of brokenness in his or her relationships. What you do with that says a lot about what you think about God.

God is able to make beauty from ashes and restore the years the locusts have eaten, and He most certainly can help you rise from the ashes of a bad decision or a bad relationship. You can't control the outside, and you can't blame your current reality or past circumstances. Jesus didn't.

Jesus didn't allow His family dynamic to define Him. He grew up in a step-family, and no one ever talks about that. No one ever talks about how it appears Jesus grew up with an overbearing mom, cantankerous siblings, and an absent earthly dad. In the midst of family dysfunction, Jesus found His identity in His heavenly Father. He was able to store up a deep reservoir of health as He spent time with the Father, as He prayed, fasted and reflected on the scriptures. When He spent time with those around Him, He poured this health into others.

Relationships are inauthentic if it's all about you, and when it's all about you, there's little to no awareness of those around you. When you meet someone, why are you more concerned with what you're going to say than who they are? You walk away, and while you hope they're impressed, you don't even remember their name. Authentic relationships have been replaced by the desire to look or sound a certain way, or be appreciated a certain way. You must enter in for the betterment of others, always learning, probing, and saying, "Tell me more about that." It must work both ways. What about your colleagues, roommates, friends or neighbors? Do you have any idea who they are? Do you talk about *their* struggles, pains, hopes and dreams?

Without a healthy relationship with God, you will never be full enough to pour out into other people. If you're in Christ, you're already loved, already accepted, already valued, already of infinite worth. Because of this, your relationships are supplements to, not substitutes for, a fulfilled life with God. You love because He loved you first, and it's not okay to live in continual brokenness.

Therefore, if anyone is in Christ, he is a new creation. The old has passed away; behold, the new has come. [93]

He calls you to love God and love people, and that's where relational health begins. Until you see what God is doing in your life to make you more like Jesus, you will never get over yourself long enough to love others. Much like Morally Discerning in which your life matters, you must realize your relationships matter too, and every relationship needs to be others-focused for it to be healthy.

WHERE DO YOU GO FROM HERE?

Here are some steps you can take to begin to grow more Relationally Healthy:

SABBATH

In the design of God, it was work then rest. For six days God worked, and on the seventh day, He rested. He didn't need a break and He certainly wasn't bored. Rather He rested to create a pattern for you. Work hard, sweat, labor well, and then take a day to rest, and it really doesn't matter when you Sabbath as long as you Sabbath. If you make it like any other day, it will just be like any other day.

---

93 2 Corinthians 5:17

You can customize your Sabbath experience and set whatever guidelines might work for you or your family. As you set your personalized plan, make it special, and hold to it as much as you can, but be flexible as life happens. Remember, rest is about the sacredness of time. It's not about the place or the things you do.

When my family is in rhythm with Sabbath, my girls are asking for it, and they know they get our faces. We make a good meal, shut off our technology, invite friends over and laugh together.

UNPLUG

No TV. No phone.

IPods, televisions and DVRs do nothing but steal your time, and relational health isn't built in a room of glowing faces. If you're always virtually connected, you communicate to those you're with that they are not as important as whatever you're looking at online.

You might consider some boundaries on the technology in your life such as a digital fast where you unplug for a set amount of time, or a digital Sabbath where you shut it down on a regular basis. While this is not possible for some occupations, for most, it's a conscious choice to be present with those around you.

SLOW DOWN

Learn to say no, create healthy boundaries, and practice the discipline of slowing down whenever possible. Create margin or space in your life, so that you're not only present, but actually enjoying those you're with. What does it look like to create unrushed, slow moments so that meaningful relationships can happen?

GOOD GOSSIP

Instead of using social media as a platform to exalt yourself, what if you used it to exalt others? Take a day and post things that make others look good. Share an experience where someone was a blessing to you or share encouraging traits you see in others.

CHAPTER 12

INCLUSIVE COMMUNITY

I MADE ENDS meet with a monthly football scholarship check of three hundred fifteen dollars, and like most college students, I never turned down a free meal.

Trent Dilfer had invited me to dinner. It was a Christian event, and they invited teammates who didn't have a personal relationship with Jesus Christ, and while I wasn't sure exactly what that meant, I knew I didn't have one. I had heard about these Christian people, and most of them knew me: attending class was completely optional, every day was Friday and the drinking typically began early. By this time in my college career, I had developed quite a reputation of stumbling out of bars like a fool, and day by day, my life was spiraling further out of control as I plunged deeper into moral darkness. I have no doubt that many wondered why on earth I was there, and truthfully, I was asking myself the same question.

At the event, I sat next to Trent, and on the other side was Brandon Bakke, the prolific three-point shooter from our basketball team. I was struck by the kindness of those present, and it actually seemed as if they cared for one another. The speaker talked about the depth of my sin. No arguments here. As the message continued, he shared about the holiness of God and how the wages of my sin was death. I had never heard this message before, at least not like this. He spoke of the love of Jesus Christ and the free gift that He offered by faith in Him. He spoke of eternal life, peace with God, and forgiveness from sin through faith in the finished work of Jesus Christ on the cross. As I listened, things began to stir inside me, and God moved in my life. I had come for free food, and I had left with a relationship with Jesus Christ, something far more fulfilling.

Here's what I didn't know at the time: Trent had told the organizers he was hopeful that I would attend, so they had begun to pray for me. We were football captains and the potential of both of us both walking with the Lord would have a profound influence on our team. Trent and Brandon, knowing I would feel awkward at a Christian event, saw me walk in, helped me find my seat and flanked me on either side. During the message, they were both praying that God would open my eyes to see the truth of Christ.

Shortly after coming to faith in Christ, I realized that growing spiritually was difficult, but growing spiritually while living in a fraternity was nearly impossible. I was in a dark place and far too weak to fight the onslaught of temptations. My young faith could be discredited in a moment of such weakness. Knowing this, Trent was intentional about helping me process how to live for Christ in a locker room, while Brandon asked me to move in with him and his three roommates, all God-fearing athletes committed to growing in their faith.

What did men of God really look like? I had read about biblical concepts but had never seen them lived out. My roommates, modeling patience and grace, helped me learn to live accountably and showed me what real friendship looked like. They showed me that I could have fun and be sober. They showed me what it meant to spend time with God, how to read my Bible and pray, how to go to church and share my faith, and how to thank God for victory and seek Him with tears when I stumbled. One day I was reading my Bible in my room. Blown away by what I was reading, I threw open my door and shouted, "This Bible is (expletive) great!" They laughed at my youthful zeal and awkwardly agreed.

• • •

"WHERE ARE YOU going?" asked John and two of his disciples. Jesus replied, "Come and see."[94]

By the age of 18, young men would search for a rabbi that they wanted to follow and ask permission to do so. The teacher would quiz the students, and if they passed, they were formally trained by the rabbi. If not, they were turned away and sent back to their father's trade. However, there was a rabbi not like the rest, and instead of men seeking Him out, He sought them. On the shores of the Sea of Galilee, He found several who were fishing.

And he said to them, "Follow me, and I will make you fishers of men." Immediately they left their nets and followed him.[95]

Follow me! Jesus called them to leave behind their livelihood, their families and their nets, and walk away. These men, most likely high school dropouts, quickly left their father's trade because He had given them a second chance.

Jesus gathered twelve disciples, and of those, three were His inner circle and one was the disciple He loved.[96] They walked together, ate together, cried and laughed together, and experienced life together. The three years Jesus spent with these men went much

---

94 See John 1:38-39
95 Matthew 4:19-20
96 See John 19:26, 21:7

deeper than the passing on of information. It was discipleship. They were invited to be *with Him*, and in the process became *like Him*. These fishermen, these so-called dropouts, learned what it meant to live in relationship with God, and their lives were marked by Him. Over time, they realized they were not only called by Him to be like Him, but also called to invite others in as well.

And Jesus came and said to them, "All authority in heaven and on earth has been given to me. Go therefore and make disciples of all nations, baptizing them in the name of the Father and of the Son and of the Holy Spirit, teaching them to observe all that I have commanded you. And behold, I am with you always, to the end of the age."[97]

Those who were invited in, invited others. On and on it went, and it changed the world.

There was incredible intentionality in the life of Christ, and there's no greater example of Inclusive Community than the incarnate God calling disciples to follow Him. The very concept of incarnation assumes that God reveals Himself most completely with face-to-face interactions, and in the life of Christ, nothing was off-limits. Rather everything was on display for the world to see. Jesus wanted them to see, firsthand, His life and work – the good and the bad. The goal of His time with these men was to make

[97] Matthew 28:18-20

them more like Him, and He knew that godliness was caught, not simply taught.

• • •

THE REST OF the story: my dad took a job in Los Angeles where he lived with his sister during the week. He couldn't find a good job where we lived, so instead of losing everything, he moved to make a living. Though he didn't move me. He kept me in school with my friends and teammates, and my dad never missed a game, often driving all day and all night to see me play. He was a wonderful dad, but he was not the best husband. After my mom, he had many girlfriends. I guess we were all trying to find some peace. Women came in and out of my life on a regular basis, and I thought, *she's nice but don't get too close. She won't be around long.* Even after the wedding ceremony to his new bride, Donna, I would introduce her as my dad's wife, never my stepmom. Although my dad had come to faith in Christ, I knew all too well old habits were hard to break, and I wasn't convinced that this marriage would last.

My dad and Donna started to grow spiritually and their home became a place of mutual encouragement. They hosted a small group and began to influence others for Christ, and as they poured themselves out into the lives of others, they grew closer together and became more and more like Jesus. Donna, no longer just my dad's wife, was now my stepmom, and the family I had longed for, I now saw in my own. We started to do what I imagined normal families to do, and I thought, *maybe, finally, we were normal.* Old things had passed away and new things had come.[98] New dads, new husbands and wives, new creations will come if

---

98 See 2 Corinthians 5:17

you're in Christ.[99] Do you believe that?

God called twelve disciples, and these guys were definitely not saints. Peter denied Him, and all of them abandoned Him except John.

> When Jesus saw his mother and the disciple whom he loved standing nearby, he said to his mother, "Woman, behold, your son!" Then he said to the disciple, "Behold, your mother!" And from that hour the disciple took her to his own home.[100]

They were all a mess, and yet He sent them out anyway, and all the while they're thinking, *who am I without you in my life?* Exactly. What do you have to offer without Jesus in your life?

You're not perfect, so quit trying to make people think you are. The charge is to become more and more like Christ, not to become Christ. It's an ongoing process and people want to see the process: the successes, the failures and the brokenness. Inviting people into your life and into your home helps them see what a Christian is like, and when you invite them in, they see it all. As you walk with Christ, they're potentially convicted in the same ways you are. You're always moving toward Him, still becoming like Him, and it's incredibly endearing and encouraging for others

99 See 2 Corinthians 5:17
100 John 19:26-27

142

to see the mess. The hope is that the mess becomes less messy over time. Living in the outer ring assumes a movement in choices, and you can't lead someone where you have never been.

Though Trent and Brandon could not articulate it at the time, what they did was model Inclusive Community. In their own way, and through their own brokenness, they invited me into their lives and showed me Christ. They intuitively recognized that the Christian life is caught, not taught, and the best way for me to experience life with Christ was to do life with others who did life with Christ.

Let Jesus live through you and invite people to follow. Let others touch it, see it and live around it because the best way for someone to express the life of Christ is to be around it. God is already putting people in your life, even today, as reminders of what He is trying to accomplish in you. Do you see them? Is there someone in your life who just needs a friend? Is there someone who needs to see Jesus in you, up close and personal?

WHERE DO YOU GO FROM HERE?

Here are some steps you can take to begin to grow more in the way of Inclusive Community:

LEVERAGE YOUR TABLE

Throughout the Gospel accounts Jesus is constantly breaking bread with those around Him. Invite someone over for dinner and simply enjoy a meal together.

Remember, Inclusive Community is an intentional invitation into your life: an invitation to be with you, to join you in doing something and to spend time together. Ordinary things, such as a slow meal with friends, can actually be sacred if you redeem the time by pointing to Jesus.

BLOCK PARTY

Holidays are a good excuse to throw a block party and find out your neighbor's name. Heat up the BBQ and invite the strangers next door over for some good food. The advantage of a block party is that the participation of the entire neighborhood makes it easier for some to join in. Perhaps neighbors who can help with the event will feel more comfortable and able to enter in. You can organize games for the kids, have a parade, do a chili cook-off, discuss the needs of the neighborhood, or just put out the lawn chairs and enjoy good conversation.

SHARED EXPERIENCE

Most women connect face to face. Put two ladies at a small table with a tasty beverage, and they can talk for hours. Most men connect shoulder to shoulder. Though they have little desire to sit and share their hearts over a baguette, they will hunt together, work out together, ride Harleys, do yard work, BBQ and eat some bacon.

So much of building healthy relationships is centered around shared experience and time spent together. While inviting someone over to *talk* can be terrifying, inviting someone over to shovel dirt might be much more comfortable. Find something you're already doing and invite someone to do it with you.

ADOPT A COLLEGE STUDENT

One way to pour into a younger generation is to invest in a college student. Invite them into your life, even if for a season. It may be for a cup of coffee or a lunch shared now and again, but know that you have something to offer. They need your wisdom, and you need their passion. The more time you spend together, the more natural the relationship will become. Maybe God will use you to shape their life, and in the process, what if they redefined retirement for you?

CHAPTER 13

BRANDED

IT WAS MIDNIGHT, and I threw open my car door and puked all over the road. Stuck is a vicious cycle and mine comes around about every three months. I hate being stuck. I don't like talking about it, and I certainly don't like writing about it. I recognize the issue has little to do with my behavior and everything to do with my heart. I would also venture to guess that if it's true in my life, it's true in yours.

When you wake up, sometimes you will be Jacob.

For the bulk of Jacob's life, it was all about him, what *he* could do, what *he* could accumulate. His very name meant trickster and deceiver. He stole his brother's birthright and father's blessing, fled home and befriended men shadier than he was. He worked for seven years to wed one girl, and was so drunk at his wedding ceremony, he slept with her sister. He then worked another seven years to wed the right girl. Jacob did whatever it took by his own strength and in his own power to make a name for himself.

When sought after by his brother and 400 men, he sent wave upon wave of peace offerings: stuff, servants and children. And once he's stripped of everything he found comfort in and left alone, a man comes to wrestle with him. It was a physical wrestling match lasting all night, and though he didn't know who the man was, Jacob never gives up. As day is about to break, the man touches the socket of Jacob's hip and blows it out. What kind of *man* can do that? With a touch of a finger, Jacob is wounded beyond repair, walking with a limp as he goes.

In that moment, Jacob realized that this was no ordinary bar fight, and whoever the man was, he had the power and authority to alter the trajectory of a man's life – to change his life and to change his very name.

And he said to him, "What is your name?" And he said, "Jacob." Then he said, "Your name shall no longer be called Jacob, but Israel, for you have striven with God and with men, and have prevailed."[101]

---

101 Genesis 32:27-28

You wake up, and sometimes you will be Jacob, and other times you will be Israel, one who strives with God. Jacob wrestled with God and now bears the scars of the beating to remind him: when you do life on your own, you're a mess.

What does God want you to do? What does He say in His word about it? It's astonishing how many Christians say, "I love Jesus," but have never really cracked the book, never really read the Bible. Do you go to church, listen to your pastor, and live off someone else's quiet time? God doesn't want to be a second tier god in your life, He wants to be everything and He deserves to be. It comes down to humble submission to God at a heart level, and you must be willfully broken and broken and broken every day. It's better to live life walking with a limp with God than to do life whole and on your own.

• • •

I GREW UP ON a five-acre farm with cattle, chickens, a pig named Wilbur, and a garage full of opportunity: broken lawnmowers, tractor parts, discarded TVs and old radios. When I was a kid, I was fascinated by how things worked and would meticulously disassemble anything I could get my hands on. I wanted to see each part, and know how it worked and how it all fit together. I spent hours in the hot Central Valley sun taking things apart; disassembling them was the easy part, putting them back together was another story.

The true uniqueness of The Anatomy of a Disciple is how each ring and each of the elements are dynamically and intimately connected to each other. They are never intended to function in isolation but are always considered inseparable from the rest.

Humbly Submitted and Biblically Formed are the foundational elements that make up the Core, and without them, authentic growth is impossible.

Humbly Submitted without being Biblically Formed:

Someone who is Humbly Submitted to God but not in the process of becoming more Biblically Formed will become emotionally driven. Over time, his or her spiritual life will be evaluated based on feeling and personal experience. Without a biblical rudder to help distinguish truth from error, decisions will be made based upon popularity or how it feels, not on the word of God. Led away and enticed by the moment, these people are "tossed to and fro by the waves and carried about by every wind of doctrine."[102]

Biblically Formed without being Humbly Submitted:

The opposite is just as dangerous. Someone who understands the text but fails to root that knowledge in a heart of humility and love will, over time, become obsessed with obedience. He or she will take more pride in being right or in winning an argument, than in being like Jesus. A rule follower who lives rightly, without humble submission to God, is unable to come to grips with grace, and often becomes a functional legalist or modern-day Pharisee.

These two elements must be present and must live in tension together to have a healthy spiritual life.

Also there must be a fundamental shift in the way you view spiritual formation. Finding your way out of the darkness is not an outward pursuit but an inward one. If you find greed, you don't have a greed problem. You have a Core problem. If you find arrogance, you don't have a pride problem. You have a Core problem. If you watch pornography, you don't have a porn problem. You have a Core problem. Instead of simply modifying behavior in the outer

102 Ephesians 4:14

rings of choices and compassions, you must look to the Core. For example, if weeds of materialism are sprouting up, you can give more, tithe more, and share your faith more, but unfortunately, that's not how authentic spiritual growth works. If your life is truly submitted to God, then you will see that life is about Him. If you read the word and are shaped by it, you will see that you're a manager of what is already His. What you have is not your own. Rather, it's God's and He has entrusted it to you. It is only then that you realize what you have is to be used for the betterment of others and not for personal indulgence. Authentic spiritual growth starts in the Core and it will not stay there; it should not stay there.

As the Core works its way outward, it will impact your choices and then your compassions in the areas or sectors of generosity, morality and relationships. For example, the choices you make in being Sacrificially Generous will overflow into the compassions you live out in Intentional Blessing, and those two elements define the Generosity Sector. Spiritual growth in the area of Morally Discerning will spill out into Culturally Engaged defining the Morality Sector, and the same goes for Relationally Healthy and Inclusive Community in respect to the Relationship Sector.

Movement outward is not without difficulty. In the sector of generosity, you will face materialism; in morality and relationships, you will face indifference and individualism, respectively. When you see a weed in your life, don't simply modify behavior. Go deeper. Do you believe that God loves you? Are you callous to what you read in scripture? Wrestle with God at your very Core and walk away broken, for only then and over time, do you stand a chance of living a life that looks like Jesus.

• • •

IF JESUS IS the goal, then you must become more like Him, but in doing so, recognize that what God has begun in you, He will be faithful to complete. God is as involved in your sanctification as He was in your salvation, and I want that to bring you hope. Your spiritual growth is still not about you; it's about what God is doing.

God, what are you doing in my life? Whatever you're doing, will you show me so that I can see it?

All authentic life change begins with God, not self-will, not suck-it-up, and most definitely, not you-can-do-it. You can't control your spiritual growth any more than you can control God. You can't fabricate it, force it or govern it because it's not yours to begin with. It's God-initiated and God-sustained, and if you submit to His leading in your life, He will help you become more like Jesus Christ over time – and it will be dirty. Dirty and painful and unpredictable and beautiful.

If we confess our sins, he is faithful and just to forgive us our sins and to cleanse us from all unrighteousness.[103]

That was the first verse I ever memorized. I was tired of keeping the outside clean while the inside was filthy, and while I never want to go back to who I was before I met Christ, I wasn't quite sure where to go from there. The Anatomy of a Disciple is for

---

103 1 John 1:9

those who find themselves living in a repetitive pattern of spiritual failure. Struggles authenticate your faith, and the afflictions you endure should be worn like a badge of honor, a reminder of who you used to be and who God wants you to be today.

I bear on my body the brand marks of Jesus.[104] God has wounded me, and I continually walk with a reminder of the brokenness.

I pastor a church in the city I grew up in, and it's really hard to run from the guy I used to be when the people I partied with in college keep showing up. I see them in the church parking lot, the sanctuary, and most of all, in the middle of teaching a message, and I'm so readily reminded of who I was: a complete moral failure.

My past is stained by poor decisions and knowing that my girls will read this book caused me great pause. What example did I want them to see? What things should they hear about and what experiences are best left unsaid? I have not always lived a life of obedience to God. I was tempted to leave out the details that might in some way embarrass them or tarnish my reputation, but the truth continued to pour out, raw and un-sanitized, and anything else would foster the inauthenticity I'm trying to eradicate. I've betrayed God and I'm ashamed of that, but I follow a long list of broken people God has chosen to redeem.

---

104 See Galatians 6:17

But by the grace of God I am what I am, and his grace toward me was not in vain.[105]

There will come a day when you are taken to be with the Lord, either in His return or your death, but until then, with God's leading, you're to identify sin in your life and uproot it viciously. As you develop greater spiritual awareness of what He is doing in your life, God will bring you to the end of yourself.

---

105 1 Corinthians 15:10

ABOUT THE AUTHOR

Brad Bell is the founding pastor of
The Well Community Church in Fresno, California,
an equipping, multisite church with four local
campuses and regional church plants,
sharing a common mission:

Helping people connect to God and to each other
in every neighborhood.

OTHER RESOURCES

The Anatomy of a Disciple:
So Many Believers. So Few Disciples.
by Dr. Rick Taylor. This and other resources can be found at
anatomyofadisciple.com.

The Anatomy of a Disciple self-assessment.
This and other resources can be found at anatomyofadisciple.com.

Made in the USA
San Bernardino, CA
17 March 2014